MW01222470

Bible Story Book for Kids: The New Testament

True Bible Stories For Children About Jesus And The New Testament Every Christian Child Should Know

Karen Jones

Copyright 2019 © Karen Jones

Legal & Disclaimer

The following document is reproduced below with the goal of providing information that is as accurate and reliable as possible.

This declaration is deemed fair and valid by both the American Bar Association and the Committee of Publishers Association and is legally binding throughout the United States.

Furthermore, the transmission, duplication or reproduction of any of the following work, including specific information, will be considered an illegal act, irrespective of if it is done electronically or in print. This extends to creating a secondary or tertiary copy of the work or a recorded copy and is only allowed with express written consent from the Publisher. All additional right reserved.

The information in the following pages is broadly considered to be a truthful and accurate account of facts, and as such, any inattention, use or misuse of the information in question by the reader will render any resulting actions solely under their purview. There are no scenarios in which the publisher or the original author of this work can be in any fashion deemed liable for any hardship or damages that may befall them after undertaking information described herein.

Additionally, the information in the following pages is intended only for informational purposes and should thus be thought of as universal. As befitting its nature, it is presented without assurance regarding its prolonged validity or interim quality. Trademarks that are mentioned are done without written consent and can in no way be considered an endorsement from the trademark holder.

Table of Contents

Introduction

Congratulations on downloading the Bible Story Book For Kids: True Bible Stories For Children About Jesus And The New Testament Every Christian Child Should Know! This Beginner's Bible is presented to educate young girls and boys about the life and ministry of the Lord Jesus Christ. It covers his Birth, Ministry, Death, Resurrection, and Ascension—as well as the resulting Christian Church that followed him. It is the Greatest Story Ever Told—about how it was possible for one man to have mankind's sins be salvaged and bring everyone to a life of following and upholding God's will.

Parents—in a world so busy, so beautiful, so interesting, and often so confusing—some of us think that we don't have time for God. However, for those who are aware of him, we can understand the peace that a prayerful life can bring to a soul. Even the little children have daily challenges and daily choices—and imparting a love of God into their heart at an early age is a wonderful gift for a fabulous life. To a child, prayer is a natural instinct. As we raise our children to do good, to live with the principles you are teaching them, it is also important to teach them the power and importance of prayer. In this world, you represent God to a young child—giving them their needs often before they even ask. God encourages all of us to teach them that it is ultimately God who supplies all of our needs.

Jesus Christ had a special fondness for children because of their innocence and willingness to accept His words without objection. God promised in the Old Testament that if parents would raise up their children in the belief of God and His Holy word, they would have a firm foundation for their entire life—and God sees us all, no matter the age, as His children. He loves all of us and only wants the best for each and every one of us.

The stories about Jesus Christ and what he did are presented in a brief, simple format, suitable to be studied with your children or read to them at night as they drift off to sleep. Simple words have been used as much as possible—with explanations for more difficult things so that the children can understand.

Lifted from the New American Standard Bible (NASB) are the italicized scriptures in this book. Some of the scriptures included in the stories have been paraphrased so that they could be clearly understood and taught.

The Bible is one of the most amazing miracles God ever performed and is written so that the youngest child to someone who studied it for his whole life can constantly find deeper and deeper levels of understanding about the God's unending compassion for all of mankind. It is our hope and prayer for this book to start a journey that will last an entire lifetime of learning about God and loving him as a personal Father, to experience a rebirth as God's creation, then eventually being with God and Jesus Christ through all eternity to come.

There exists a plethora of literature on this topic on the internet—I genuinely appreciate your decision to pick this one! Rest assured that all possible work was done to guarantee that this book is as jam-packed and abundant in details as it possibly can. Enjoy!

1. A Visit by an Angel

*And behold, you will conceive in your womb
and bear a son, and you shall name Him Jesus.
He will be great and will be called the Son of the
Most High; and the Lord God will give Him the
throne of His father David, and He will reign
over the house of Jacob forever, and His
kingdom will have no end."*
(Luke 1:31-33)

A long, long time ago, in a tiny county called Israel, there was a beautiful young lady whose name was Mary. She lived in a little farming village called Nazareth. All the lands around Lake Kinnereth had roll hills, little fishing villages, farms, and a few bigger towns that were collectively called the Land of Galilee. The people were peaceful, worked hard, loved God, and went to their church called a synagogue to worship God and hear the readings of the ancient scrolls that held the words of all the prophets.

In the ancient writings of the prophets (what we now call the Old Testament), mankind was said to be earthed by the Father Almighty—but the foremost of his kind, Adam, sinned against God, which gave rule over the earth to a fallen angel. The angel was originally called Lucifer, but he came to be called the Devil—or Satan. For thousands of years, Satan brought death and destruction to everyone, and the people cried over and over for a Savior to save the world from its sins to ultimately have them come back to the Father. Ancient prophets all talked about this man who would one day come, and the people waited through the years for him to be born.

God had chosen a man named Abram as His creation's father and given a promised land to his children forever. The children of Abraham grew and went through many adventures and mishaps, which became recorded in what we call today the *Old Testament* and what the Jews call the *Torah*. It was recorded that God promised to Eve that a child would be born one day that would rule the world. Throughout time, all the prophets saw his coming and swore for a king who'd save mankind. Mary was smart and kind and raised by her parents to love God and to know His magnificent works and creations for her kind, the Judeans, written about in the ancient scrolls in their church called a synagogue; like Joseph saving the Israelites from the famine; or like Moses parting the Red Sea the morning after the first Passover. Her hometown was mostly a quiet farming town—full of people who worked hard, went to their church every weekend, and raised their families according to the laws of God.

However, in those days, Nazareth and all of Israel was ruled over by a mean, far-away kingdom called Rome. Even though Rome was far away, they had a governor that controlled the country and had many soldiers that bossed around the people and made them pay taxes to the mean Roman emperor whose name was Caesar Augustus—and a king he appointed over Israel, an even meaner man named King Herod. Nobody in Nazareth liked either one of them and hated having to pay taxes so that King Herod could build things for Emperor Augustus and for himself.

One big city in Galilee, next to the lake, was called Caesarea Philippi, having been built by the Romans with the Jewish tax money to honor the Roman emperor. Another big city, west of Galilee, called Caesarea, was a port being built by King Herod on the Mediterranean coast, with statues of Emperor Augustus and King Herod all around the city—and the people there worshipped all kinds of other gods.

This Mary loved a young man in the village called Joseph. Joseph was a carpenter—he built things out of wood like tables and chairs and many other things. He was respected in his village because he always concentrated on his work and built the best things for the people to use in their houses. Joseph loved Mary very much as well—and so, one day, he went to Mary's parents and asked if they would let him Mary marry him. They were happy and said yes because they knew that Joseph was a fine young man, successful in his business, and would be able to take good care of their daughter and bring them beautiful grandchildren as well.

Mary was very happy to find out that her parents said she could marry Joseph, and both began to prepare for the wedding. Joseph had to fix up his house so that he could have room when Mary moved in, and Mary had to prepare her wedding dress and buy special jewelry to wear in her hair on her wedding day.

One night, when Mary was laying in her bed thinking about her upcoming wedding and how wonderful it would be to be married to Joseph, she was surprised when a man appeared out of nothing in her bedroom. "Don't be scared Mary— I am not here to hurt you. I am an angel, and my name is Gabriel. God sent me, and I have come to tell you something very important."

Mary knew about angels from the ancient texts they read in church and immediately calmed down. "Yes, angel Gabriel, I understand. What have you come to tell me?"

The angel said, "I am to tell you that you are going to be pregnant and have a baby—and he is a very special child. He will become the King of Israel, like your ancestor King David, and he will rule the land forever."

Now, Mary had a puzzled look on her face and thought about places in the ancient scrolls that promised a king would be born someday that would rule over Israel like a lion and would be loving and wonderful and not at all like the

Romans who were always mean to them and took pride in bossing them around.

However, Mary was puzzled by the fact that she was engaged to Joseph but not married yet, so she asked the angel how it was possible that she could become pregnant and have a baby.

Gabriel told her not to worry—that God was going to make her pregnant and that nothing was impossible for God. God wanted a son that He could call his own. He also told Mary that her cousin, Elizabeth, who lived in another town, was pregnant, too, even though she was too old to have a baby.

Mary accepted what the angel said and replied to Gabriel, "Behold the handmaid of the Lord. Be it unto me according to your word." At that very instant, Mary became pregnant with God's baby, and the angel Gabriel disappeared.

Mary soon went to Elizabeth's village and found out that yes, as the angel had told her, Elizabeth was very pregnant. When they saw each other and hugged hello, both babies in their bellies kicked their mommies, leaping for joy! Mary remained in her friend's home within the next 3 months, helping Elizabeth around the house so that she could be comfortable and have a happy baby.

Elizabeth told Mary all about what had happened to her. She had been very sad because she thought she was cursed, having been married for many years but never had been able to have a baby. The same angel Gabriel came to her husband, Zacharias, who was one of the priests in the Temple. Gabriel came while he was in the Temple and promised that she would become pregnant and that they would have a son. The angel said that he would become the messenger to pave the way for the new king who was coming after him, and he was to name the baby John. However, Zacharias didn't believe what the angel had said, and he was made speechless.

While she was there helping Elizabeth, Mary's own belly began to grow bigger and bigger, too. After the three months, Mary eventually had to go home—but when she came to say hi to her boyfriend, Joseph, he realized that she was pregnant, and he knew it wasn't his because they weren't married yet. He was very upset with Mary and thought for days and days what he should do about it. He loved Mary very much, but he thought he should call off the wedding because she was pregnant with someone else's baby. He thought maybe he should break off the engagement.

Then one night, Joseph was sleeping and tossing and turning in his bed, and he had a dream. The same angel, Gabriel, came to him in the dream and assured him that the baby was God's baby and that he needed to go ahead and marry Mary as soon as possible.

And so, as soon as the arrangements could be finished, Joseph and Mary had a big celebration before the whole town of Nazareth, and they were married. They were very happy and kept the secret from everyone that she was pregnant on her wedding day.

Now, several months later, Elizabeth was finally ready to have her baby. After 8 days, they had him christened at the Temple. When he was asked what the child's name would be, he wrote on a tablet that he would be called John, as he still couldn't speak. Immediately, he was able to talk and praise God.

2. Jesus Is Born

She gave birth to her firstborn, a son. She wrapped him in cloths and placed him in a manger because there was no guest room available for them. . . . But the angel said to them, "Do not be afraid—for behold, I bring you good news of great joy, which will be for all the people—for today, in the city of David, there has been born for you a Savior, who is Christ the Lord.

(Luke 2:7. 10-11)

After Joseph and Mary were married, a Roman soldier came to Nazareth and told everyone in the village that they have to travel at a certain time to the town their ancestors came from to be counted for a census. A census is a list of names, where they lived, and what they did for a living. Emperor Augustus had wanted to know all the names of the people he rules in Israel. Both Joseph and Mary were descended from King David, whose hometown was a little village near Jerusalem called Bethlehem, so that was where they knew they had to go.

Mary was very pregnant, close to having the baby—but they had to go, or they would get into a lot of trouble. Hence, they packed up a horse, with a cart behind it, and Joseph drove the horse while pulling Mary in the cart behind him. A bunch of other families from Nazareth went with them. People didn't usually travel alone in those days because of dangers that could happen on a trip. When they got close to Bethlehem, some of the other families went off to the towns and villages they had to go to, but some of them stayed with Joseph and Mary all the way to Bethlehem.

When they got there, Joseph found a shady spot for Mary to wait, and he went to all the places in town that had rooms for visitors—but everyone was already full of people coming to Bethlehem for the census. He looked and looked all day, but he couldn't find a single empty room. He told everyone that his wife was very pregnant, but they couldn't help him at all.

Finally, at the last place he tried, Joseph told the man running the Inn that he desperately needed a room because his wife was very pregnant and about to have her baby. The man told him that his Inn was already full, but they could sleep in a stable he owned for his horses and donkeys and sheep. Joseph gladly accepted the offer so that he could get Mary into any place rather than laying in the cart.

The stable had a large open area in the middle, which is called a manger—full of hay and water and tools for feeding the animals, with stalls all around that caged the animals in. The stable smelled sweet with the hay, and the man who owned it had kept it clean. Joseph helped Mary out of the cart and into the manger and made a bed for her to lay in out of the hay so that he could rest after the long trip there. The nice man who owned the house and the stable brought them food and water while they were his guests.

The lines to sign the census list was very long, and they had to wait a few days until they could sign it. While they were waiting, one evening, Mary began to feel her baby moving, and Mary started to have the baby. Soon, the little baby boy was born, and Joseph took the baby and cleaned it off.

Then, Joseph took the baby and wrapped a cloth around it that had been soaked in water and salt, to show God that he was committing the baby to Him and that he would do his best to raise up the baby to be kind and honest and have a love for God always. The cloth, which was called swaddling clothes, was only wrapped around the baby for a few moments while the parents would pray for the baby to be safe and healthy and happy. It was a tradition that the Jews of the time did for all newborn babies. He remembered what the angel Gabriel had told both—that God had said to call him Jesus, so Joseph did just that and laid the baby down into Mary's arms.

During the moments when the Son of God was being delivered, an angel by the name of Gabriel appeared in the hills that surround Bethlehem. There was a group of young men sitting around a campfire, watching over their herds of sheep sleeping in the fields. The land was still full of wolves and other animals that loved to eat sheep, so they had to be guarded day and night by shepherds. These young men were all devoted to God and went to church every week to worship him.

The angel appeared to the shepherds, with a radiant glow all around him, and the shepherds became scared at the sight because they had never seen an angel before. "Do not worry," Gabriel said, "because I have come to tell you some great news."

"Tonight, a baby was born in Bethlehem who is the Messiah God promised would come to Israel, who will become the King of Kings. You go to the Inn in Bethlehem, and you will find the baby still wrapped up in the swaddling clothes, lying in the manger with his mother, Mary."

Just then, all around them, many other angels appeared, praising God about the baby. They all said together, "Glory to God in the highest, and on earth peace—Goodwill toward men."

After all the angels disappeared, the shepherds immediately ran into Bethlehem and found the Inn and went into the stable—and just like the angel Gabriel had told them, they arrived just when Joseph was putting the baby into Mary's arms, still wrapped in its swaddling clothes. They were so excited, that they hugged Joseph and kissed Mary and the baby on their cheeks—then, they praised God that the new king had been born. They ran to tell all their friends that they had been visited by angels and seen the newborn baby who would be the King. All the people who heard the story were amazed and hopeful that the king that they had hoped for was born.

The next week, they had their baby christened in one of the temples of Jerusalem. They bought two young pigeons outside to be sacrificed in the Temple. When they were there, they encountered two very old people who had prayed for all their lives that they wouldn't die before seeing the promised King from God. Their names were Simon and Anna, and both of them were given the Holy Spirit and prophesied wonderful things when they saw the baby. Simon took the baby and prayed to God in front of Joseph and Mary, saying: "Now, Lord, You are releasing Your bond-servant to depart in peace, according to Your word; for my eyes have seen Your salvation, which You have prepared in the presence of all peoples, A LIGHT OF REVELATION TO THE GENTILES, and the glory of Your people in Israel."

Anna, an 84-year old woman, was also there to watch and praise the newborn. Joseph and Mary's eyes opened wide to see and hear these things said about their baby.

3. The Bright Star and The Three Visitors

Now, after Jesus was born in Bethlehem of Judea, in the days of Herod the king, magi from the east arrived in Jerusalem and said, "Where is He who has been born King of the Jews? For we saw His star in the east and have come to worship Him."
(Matthew 2:1-2)

After the baby was born, Joseph was able to sign the census and take Mary and the baby back to Nazareth. At the same time, far away, a group of men who studied the stars had been watching wonderful things happening. Stars were lining up in ways they had never seen before—the king planet Jupiter lining up with the constellation Regulus and the constellation Leo, the lion. They wondered what it all meant.

Hundreds of years before, the astronomers of a country called Persia had been taught by a very wise man named Daniel, that someday there would be born in Israel a king whose kingdom would never end. God revealed His entire plan for mankind in the stars, in their formations called constellations, and the movements of the heavenly bodies. The astronomers who watched for these signs were called Magi because they had special secrets like magicians. They all knew and trusted that Daniel received these things from God, because God had shown Daniel secrets in the king's dreams, and protected him when he was cast into a lion's den. Every generation of Magi taught the young astronomers all about the prophecies of Daniel and watched the skies every night for the heavenly ciphers of the King's arrival.

Now, finally, it was here! Sign after the sign

appeared in the stars, and they were convinced that the king had been born. "We must go worship him," they said to themselves. They packed up their camels full of all sorts of precious items to give to the newborn king. They were gold and rare spices called frankincense and myrrh.

After many days, the Magi finally had prepared for the long trip from Persia to the capital of Israel, Jerusalem. They went to the king of Israel, a very mean man named King Herod, and asked to see the newborn king. Herod was very mad and said I don't know anything about a newborn king. I am the King of Israel. Where did you hear that some other king was born?"

The magi told old King Herod about all the signs in the skies, and the prophecies about the king who would be born and rule forever. They told him about a prophecy in the ancient scrolls that the baby came from Bethlehem, David's city and that it happened about two months before.

Since they didn't get any help from mean old King Herod, they got back on their camels and traveled the short distance to from Jerusalem to Bethlehem and asked about the newborn king. Many of the townspeople knew of it, from the wondrous stories told to them by the shepherds about that night. The townspeople told the Magi that the parents were only visiting Bethlehem for the census and that they had returned to their own village of Nazareth.

Knowing now where to go, the Magi took their camels again and traveled north to the Sea of Galilee, and found the town of Nazareth, and the house of Joseph the Carpenter there. Joseph let them in, and there they found the young child playing on the floor with his mother. Baby Jesus was now almost two months old.

The Magi told Joseph and Mary that they had come from very far away, to honor the newborn king and to bring him presents. They unpacked the camels and brought in jars full of gold coins, and spices, and rich cloth for the baby. Mary was simply amazed how many times and ways God had shown her and Joseph that this little boy was the future king that all the prophets had promised in the past!

But after the Magi left, the angel Gabriel warned him to take the baby to Egypt, as King Herod was searching for the young child that would become a future king. King Herod had demanded the death of every child below the age of 2 living in Bethlehem. The Magi had told King Herod approximately how old the boy was at that time. Hundreds of young babies were taken from their parents and killed. But since the boy he was searching for had returned to Nazareth, the angel warned Joseph that King Herod would be looking for them there next! So, Joseph took Mary and the young child, and immediately packed up their things and traveled down into Egypt. It was just a little while until King Herod died, and they were able to return to Nazareth without fearing for the life of Jesus.

4. Jesus Is Lost

Then, after three days, they found Him in the temple, sitting in the midst of the teachers, both listening to them and asking them questions.
(Luke 2:46)

Now, Joseph and Mary took great care raising the child Jesus. Because Joseph was a successful carpenter, he made a good income to raise his family, and they were able to use the gold and rare spices when they had to buy things—and Mary had other babies, boys, and girls—among them were James, Joseph, Jude, Simon, and their sisters, too.

Jesus was just like other regular children growing up. He had toys and friends to play with. He had to learn to read and go to school and to church to become a smart child.

Joseph and Mary followed all the laws of Moses and raised their family well, taking them to the synagogue every weekend—and on three special holy days, they all traveled together to the big city, Jerusalem. The Jews had special holidays called Passover in the spring, Pentecost in the summer, and Tabernacles in the fall. All Judeans were supposed to at least come to Jerusalem on those holidays and worship at the Temple, a sort of big church, to honor God by following the laws of Moses. Joseph and Mary went every year according to the law of Moses.

In that time, it was dangerous to travel alone, so families would get together into a large group, called a caravan, and the men would ride together with the other men, the women together with the women, and the children together with all the other children. Of course, the children traveled with one or more babysitters who would make sure they were taken care of. At night, the families would all be reunited to share their meals and night time together.

During the Passover in Jesus' 12th year, they visited Jerusalem. The beautiful Temple in Jerusalem, built by King Herod on the site of the earlier Temple built by King Solomon, was a wonder to behold, and filled with people from all over. It was built out of white limestone blocks, with an outer courtyard for anyone to come into, and an inner courtyard that only Jews could go into, and a special room that is solely accessible to the High Priest. There, the High Priest sacrificed annually in the Holy of Hollies for the sins of all Jewish people to be forgiven.

At the feast of Passover, extended families got together for wonderful meals, lambs and unleavened bread and tart greens to remind them all the miracle of God saving the people by Moses, when the angel of Death killed all the first-born Egyptian children and passed over Israelite children. It also remembered Red Sea's miracles by parting as they left Egypt and went to Mount Sinai. They went to the Temple and heard the blessings of the priests, and saw the High Priest go into the Holy of Holiness to ask that God forgave all the sins of the Jews from the previous year.

When the feast days were over, Joseph and the men of his village gathered everyone together for the long trip back home. Once again, the men traveled together, the women together, and all the children in the rear. They traveled all day long and had gotten part way home when they stopped to camp for the evening.

Mary went to where all the children were gathered, and found her sons, James, Joseph, Jude and Simon, and their sisters, but where was Jesus? Nobody had seen him, and the babysitters had not realized that he was gone.

"Oh no," Mary cried, "We have lost our precious son, the promised King." She started to cry and shake, remembering all the things that the angel had said about him, but Joseph calmed her down. "We will go back together to find him," he told her.

The next morning, they left the camp early, after asking a friend to take care of the rest of their family while they searched for their older brother. As quickly as they could, Joseph and Mary returned to Jerusalem, reaching it at nightfall. There was no way to search the crowded city at night, so they found a room and nervously slept together.

The next morning, they went searching for Jesus. They went from house to house, asking where there lost son might be. Finally, one of the men in the city said, "I think I saw a young boy who sounds like him at the Temple yesterday." Joseph and Mary ran to the Temple as fast as they could, through narrow alleys clogged with people. When they finally got there, they asked the Temple guards if they had seen the boy. They said, "yes," there is a boy about that age meeting with the high priests right now."

Joseph and Mary were led into a meeting room, where they finally found their son. He was surrounded by the old priests of the Temple, called Pharisees and Sadducees, asking them questions about God and about the promises of a future King. The temple priests were also asking him questions and astonished to hear the young boy answer difficult questions about the Law and the history of the Israelites.

When Jesus noticed that his parents were in the room watching him, he ran over to them and gave them both a big hug. Mary was crying tears of joy for finding him. Joseph began to scold Jesus for running off and being separated from the rest of their group. Mary asked him "Why did you run off. We were both so worried that we would never find you."

Jesus looked at his parents and told them, "Dad, Mom, don't you realize that I should be doing what my Father told me to do?" To this, they didn't fully understand what he meant, because he was talking about God, but they were very glad to have him back. So, they returned to Nazareth

Jesus continued to grow into a young man and then an adult as an assistant to his father in the carpenter's shop, helping his mother, being a part of the community, going to the synagogue every weekend, being friends to others. He went to the classes where he and all the other children of the town learned from the old scrolls about Abraham and Moses and all the prophets, and the rise and fall of the Jewish people into different evil kings. And so, he grew up with everyone thinking that he was a wonderful young man.

5. Jesus Is Baptized

After being baptized, Jesus came up immediately from the water; and behold, the heavens were opened, and he saw the Spirit of God descending like a dove and lighting on Him, and behold, a voice out of the heavens said, "This is My Beloved Son, in whom I am well-pleased."
(Matthew 3:16-17)

J esus grew to become a young man of thirty years old, finally accepted as a mature adult in the eyes of the Jewish community. He had heard that his cousin John was becoming quite a celebrity around the country. John had gone out into the desert for months, living on what God provided for him. He wore an animal skin, tied with a leather belt, and lived on nothing but locusts and honey.

When he returned from the desert, he began to travel all over the country, teaching about a coming King. Some people even thought that John was the Messiah they had been looking for. But John told them that he was only the forerunner of the Messiah, that he wasn't even worthy to tie the shoes of the person coming after him.

The people of Israel had been spiritually dead for hundreds of years. The last prophet before John the Baptist was named Malachi. Malachi prophesied that "I will send you a messenger, and he will prepare the way for the Lord." But for four hundred years there hadn't been a real prophet in Israel. John preached about the coming Messiah, calling the people of his time a "generation of snakes".

He also told people that God was telling him they should be baptized in the Jordan River, to signify to God their return to worshipping him. John baptized with water but taught that soon a new king would arise who baptized with the Holy Spirit. People began to follow him around, to listen to him teaching about all the old prophets who had promised that someday a new King of Israel would come along and that this king was near. At that moment, John didn't realize that it was his own cousin Jesus he was prophesying about.

God told Jesus to go find John, and he found out where John was and went down to the Jordan River. He sat in the grass and listened to John preaching to a crowd around him about God and all the miracles that God had done for Israel over the centuries, and about their need to return to God. When John was done preaching, he offered to baptize anyone who wanted to come forward.

Jesus stood up and walked toward him, and John saw his cousin coming and smiled. They hugged each other, and Jesus told John, "I would like to be baptized." John looked at Jesus and told him, "No, cousin, you should be baptizing me!"

Jesus looked deep into John's eyes and told him, "Dear John, there will come a time that I will be able to baptize—but right now is your time, and it's in front of God's eyes that you are to fulfill your destiny so that I might be able to later fulfill mine."

So, John led him out into the river and helped to submerge Jesus into the water. When Jesus stood up, water dripped off his hair and his chin and his clothes, they saw what looked like a white dove coming down from heaven and landed on Jesus's head and disappeared. Then everyone in the crowd heard a loud voice coming above that said, "This is my beloved Son, in whom I am well pleased."

The crowd was astonished. John and Jesus looked at each other and smiled, and then John hugged Jesus tightly. At the moment that the spirit landed upon Jesus, he was able to communicate directly with God and begin his own righteous ministry.

From then on, John would teach to all his followers that his cousin Jesus was the "Lamb of God, who would take away all the sins of the world." He told his followers that they should be ready to follow this Jesus instead of him because Jesus surely was the Son of God.

6. Jesus Chooses His Apostles

Now as Jesus was walking by the Sea of Galilee, He saw two brothers, Simon who was called Peter, and Andrew his brother, casting a net into the sea; for they were fishermen. And He said to them, "Follow Me, and I will make you fishers of men."
(Matthew 4:18-19)

God led Jesus into the desert and lived there for forty days, praying about the ministry that he was to begin, working in his mind all the scriptures about his future and about all thing things he had learned growing up. Near the end of that time, Satan, the devil, came to Jesus and tried to tempt him to not start his ministry. He tempted Jesus with food first because Jesus had been living in the desert so long. He tried to trick Jesus into thinking he could jump off a high cliff and that God would send angels to save him. Then, the devil told him he could make him the King of the World, richer beyond his wildest imagination—if he would only worship the Devil. The devil could do this honestly because Adam had given him the control of the whole world and all its riches when Adam sinned. Jesus answered every temptation with the Word of God—and eventually, the Devil backed off and went away.

Now, after Jesus returned from the desert, God told him that he needed a team to work with him. He began to look around for people that could follow him and learn from him. He knew that he would have a lot of followers, who he could teach about God and God's will for man, but he needed some special people around him to whom he could teach the deeper secrets of God, and who would carry on his words after he was gone.

He met two of John's followers, who believed what John had taught about Jesus. Jesus asked, "Why are you following me?"

The men answered, "Where do you live? We want to come to hear more about God from you." The two men followed Jesus to his house, and it was already late afternoon, so they ate and talked about God all night. The next morning, one of the men, whose name was Andrew, told Jesus that he wanted to go find his brother, who would love to hear all about God too.

Andrew went to Jesus' house with his brother Simon. Jesus told him that he would call Simon by the name of Cephas, which was Peter in English and meant a tiny little pebble. Peter was a man full of emotions, he would be a strong believer one day, and a coward the next. One day, he was bound to forsake Jesus. That was why Jesus called him Peter because he would blow hot one day, and cold the next day. Andrew and Peter and another disciple stayed with Jesus all day, talking about wonderful things.

The next day, Jesus began by leaving his house one morning in Nazareth, and taking a peaceful walk to Lake Kinnereth, talking to God and his three new friends along the way. It was a beautiful day, with a soft breeze blowing over the lake. Fishing boats bobbed up and down on the little ripples of the lake, and many boats were already out in the middle of the lake with their fishermen.

The four of them walked together along the seashore and saw a group of people in a boat close to shore. Everyone knew each other in this little fishing town, so Jesus recognized the fisherman Zebedee, and his two sons James and John, and some servants who were helping them. They were busy fixing holes that had torn in their fishing webs. Jesus asked for their attention, and so they rowed back to the shore and talked with James and John about God, too. They told Zebedee that they were going off with Jesus to talk about God, and Zebedee allowed them to go.

They came to the next little fishing village, called Bethsaida, which was where Andrew and Peter's house was. One of the brothers ran to find a friend he had, named Philip. Philip was so excited to hear about God and saw how happy his friends were with Jesus. So, he ran off to find another friend of theirs, whose name was Nathaniel.

One by one, Jesus found friends who would not only be followers of his words, disciples but be fully committed to Jesus and to whom he could teach the innermost secret of God. Those he called apostles, and there were twelve of them. Because these men already deeply believed in God, Jesus was able to trust them and teach them the deeper mysteries about God. For the common people, he could only teach them the basics, which they could understand. They were Peter, Andrew, Matthew, James, Phillip, Thomas, John, ... Bartholomew, James the son of Alpheus, Simon Zelotes, Jude the brother of James, and Judas Iscariot. The first eleven of these men all came from the Galilee region, but Judas came from a town named Kerioth, close to the Mediterranean Sea.

7. Water into Wine

Jesus said to them, "Fill the waterpots with water." So they filled them up to the brim. And He said to them, "Draw some out now and take it to the headwaiter." So they took it to him. When the headwaiter tasted the water, which had become wine
(John 2:7-9)

After he had assembled his team, Jesus began to visit all the Jewish places of worship called synagogues around the Galilee to preach. When he went to the synagogue in his own town, Nazareth, it was his turn to read from the scrolls. That was a practice then—each man took turns to read from a scroll every week.

Jesus read from the scroll of Isaiah:

The Spirit of the Lord GOD is upon me
Because the LORD has anointed me
To bring good news to the afflicted;
He has sent me to bind up the brokenhearted,
To proclaim liberty to captives
And freedom to prisoners;
To proclaim the favorable year of the LORD
(Isaiah 61:1-2)

This statement from the prophecy of Isaiah was a good summary of what his whole ministry was going to be about. Jesus stopped before the end of the verse, which said, "and the day of vengeance of our God" because that was only yet to come.

One day, Jesus was invited to a large nuptial in the nearby village of Cana. Jesus's mother, Mary, was also invited to the party. Weddings in those days were large, joyous occasions that often lasted several days, and included a lot of food and wine.

Sometime during the party, Mary approached Jesus to tell him they'd run out of wine. He first told his mother that it wasn't his responsibility to get more wine, because it wasn't his wedding, but they told her that he would fix it anyway. Mary went over to the men who were serving all the guests, and pointed to her son Jesus and told them, "My son can help, do whatever he tells you to do."

Then Jesus walked over to the servants and told them to go get six big clay pots and fill them up to the very top with water. Jesus talked to God and when God told him it was ok, Jesus told the head servant to dip a cup into one of the pots and fill a cup and take it to the father of the bride. The servant did as he was asked, and the father sipped the water, which had turned into the most splendid wine. Nobody except the servants knew that the pots had only been filled with water, not wine.

The father of the bride called over the bridegroom, his new son-in-law, and told the crowd that they had all started off drinking the lesser wine, but now the finest wine was in the room. He did not know it, but the father of the bride was really talking about Jesus, the real fine wine in the room! This was the first of the miracles that Jesus would perform in his ministry.

8. Jesus Calms the Storm

He said to them, "Why are you afraid, you men of little faith?" Then He got up and rebuked the winds and the sea, and it became perfectly calm. The men were amazed, and said, "What kind of a man is this, that even the winds and the sea obey Him?"
(Matthew 8:26-27)

One day, Jesus and his apostles had been teaching large crowds of people around the city of Capernaum, a city much bigger than his hometown of Nazareth, which was also alongside the Sea of Kinnereth. Jesus went to the synagogue and preached there about the deliverance of God with great power.

A possessed man came out from the crowd. The devil has thousands of devil spirits under him, who are able to possess the minds of many who are not given to God. God originally created the angels and put three angels in charge of them, Michael, Gabriel, and Lucifer. Michael was the angel who fights for Gods people. Gabriel was the angel who brings great messages to people. Lucifer was created to be the Angel of Light. When the angel Lucifer revolted against God, thinking he was as good as God, God cast him down to the earth and Lucifer acquired a third of his fellows when he was cast to the earth.

"How you have fallen from heaven,
O star of the morning, son of the dawn!
You have been cut down to the earth,
You who have weakened the nations!
But you said in your heart,
'I will ascend to heaven;
I will raise my throne above the stars of God,
And I will sit on the mount of assembly
In the recesses of the north.
'I will ascend above the heights of the clouds;
I will make myself like the Most High.
Nevertheless you will be thrust down to Sheol,

To the recesses of the pit.
(Isaiah 14:12-15)

God is only perfect Love. He doesn't hurt or kill anyone. But the devil only lies, kills and destroys. The devil's angels worship the devil like he was God, and they followed his orders around the earth. They are the ones who hurt and kill, to make them sick and die, who make men do evil things.

The possessed man boldly walked up to Jesus and said, "Leave us alone Jesus. Are you here to destroy us? I know who you are, the Holy One of God." The man didn't know who Jesus was, but the devil spirit inside him did. Jesus demanded the departure of the bad element—and so it immediately did, and the man was healed of the torment the spirit was putting him through. God's spirit working through people who believe him are much more powerful than these evil spirits, and if they are ordered to leave someone, they have to go.

The people in the synagogue were astonished to see a man with such power. Word was spread around Capernaum, and many people came to see him and hear his words. They brought many sick people with them, and Jesus was able to call upon God to heal them all. It was a wonderful time, with people smiling and hugging each other seeing the many miracles that Jesus performed.

His apostle, Peter, asked Jesus to come to his house there because his mother was sick. The crowd followed Jesus and his apostles down the street and then stood outside while Jesus and the twelve apostles went into the house. Jesus went over to the lady, and held her hands, and prayed for her, and she was immediately healed. She felt so perfect that she got up and began cooking dinner for all of them.

The crowd of people kept calling for Jesus to come back out, and when he did, he saw it had grown larger, and many other sick people were there hoping to be healed. Jesus taught and healed them for many hours until it was dark.

Jesus was getting tired, but the crowd just kept growing and growing. Jesus told one of his apostles to go find a boat to borrow, so they could get away from the crowd and get a little rest. A boat was found, and they all climbed aboard it, and Jesus fell deeply asleep.

Suddenly, in the middle of the lake, and far from any shore, a strong wind came up, and the waves increased, and the boat began to rock up and down. Water splashed into the bottom of the boat. The apostles were scared, thinking the boat would tip over and they would all drown, but Jesus was peacefully sleeping.

They got so scared, they finally shook Jesus until he woke up. They told him, "Jesus, Jesus, help us. We are all going to die out here!"

Jesus looked at them and shook his head. They had just seen all sorts of people be healed the day before, and now they are all scared. "Why are you afraid. Oh, ye of little faith", he said to them." They still didn't really believe that God could do anything.

The Jesus walked over to the edge of the boat and bowed his head and prayed to God. Immediately the wind stopped, and the sea became calm again. The men shook their heads in amazement, whispering to each other, "What kind of man is that, that ever the winds and the sea obey him." Jesus just smiled and them and went back to bed.

Jesus continued touring around Galilee, preaching and teaching and healing the sick. But he also had caught the attention of the religious leaders of the day, who began to question if a man had the right to forgive sins, to heal the sick, and so on. They were afraid because of the obvious power of God that Jesus demonstrated.

In those days, the priests really didn't love God

or follow Him. They lived well off the donations that people paid to the Temple and objected to anyone who might threaten to take away their easy life. There were two main groups of priests, called the Pharisees and the Sadducees. They made up all sorts of silly rules for the people to follow, which were not really based on the old prophets. They told people what they could and could not eat, or wear, or do, but it was all just to control them. Many times in the ministry of Jesus, he told them that they were sinning against God, because they were supposed to be helping the people but were really only using them.

9. Sermon on the Mount

When Jesus saw the crowds, He went up on the mountain; and after He sat down, His disciples came to Him. He opened His mouth and began to teach them...
(Matthew 5:1-2)

After he began preaching all around the region of Galilee, where Nazareth was, more and more people began to travel from all over the country to hear him. He taught large crowds in the synagogues of the Jews, who met every Saturday. He taught crowds in the markets, on the streets, and people in their homes. Soon, people started to come from as far away as Jerusalem and even from across Jordan River and in other countries to hear him speak and to watch his miracles.

One day, a massive crowd formed that was so big

that people in the back couldn't even see or hear what was happening. Jesus told them all to follow him, and he left the city he was in and walked to a high hill, where he could stand above all the people and they could all see and hear him. Jesus stood, but everyone sat down in the grass and stared at him.

Jesus began to preach of all the things of God, in a loving but firm way. He began by setting forth general guidelines or rules for people to follow, so they could find Godly happiness in their lives:

"Blessed are the poor in spirit, for theirs is the kingdom of heaven.

Blessed are those who mourn, for they shall be comforted.

Blessed are the gentle, for they shall inherit the earth.

Blessed are those who hunger and thirst for righteousness, for they shall be satisfied. Blessed are the merciful, for they shall receive mercy. Blessed are the pure in heart, for they shall see

God.

Blessed are the peacemakers, for they shall be called sons of God.

Blessed are those who have been persecuted for the sake of righteousness, for theirs is the kingdom of heaven.

Blessed are you when people insult you and persecute you, and falsely say all kinds of evil against you because of Me.

Rejoice and be glad, for your reward in heaven is great; for, in the same way, they persecuted the prophets who were before you."

(Matthew 5:2-12)

Then Jesus continued all day, speaking for hours about the Laws of Moses, and the Ten Commandments, and how people had twisted the laws to make them all easier to get past. Jesus taught them to be peaceful, and loving, forgiving even someone who was mean to you. Jesus told them to let their light shine for the whole world to see it.

Jesus' teachings were different from the angry words of the ministers who taught in the synagogues, who were often mad and taught people to fear and hate. Jesus's words were so much kinder and made God seem to them more as a loving God—than a God who made people sick or die.

He also scolded people who stand out in the street corners, praying for everyone to see how important they think they are, and told them to instead go into a closet and talk to God person to person. He even taught them an example of a prayer to say, just between them and God:

"Our Father who is in heaven,
Hallowed be Your name.
Your kingdom come.
Your will be done,
On earth as it is in heaven.
Give us this day our daily bread.
And forgive us our debts, as we also have
forgiven our debtors.

And do not lead us into temptation, but deliver us from evil. For Yours are the kingdom and the power and the glory forever. Amen."

(Matthew 6:9-13)

By the end of the day, everyone was smiling and hugging and some were even crying, having learned that they were listening to a man who spoke directly from God's heart.

10. Jesus Forgives and Heals a Paralyzed Man

And they came, bringing to Him a paralytic, carried by four men. Being unable to get to Him because of the crowd, they removed the roof above Him; and when they had dug an opening, they let down the pallet on which the paralytic was lying. And Jesus seeing their faith said to the paralytic, "Son, your sins are forgiven.
(Mark 2:3-6)

J esus and his apostles went back to the town of Capernaum again—and soon, another large crowd had assembled around the house he was at. So many people came to hear him preach to the point that the whole house was filled, and people pushed into all the doors and the windows of the house to hear him.

While he was preaching, four men came to the house with a bed carrying another man. This man was paralyzed, and he couldn't walk or even talk. His friends wanted him to be healed by Jesus, but they couldn't even get close enough to the house to hear him, let alone get to Jesus and hope that he can heal their friend.

In those days, many of the houses had flat roofs, covered over with wood and straw. One of the men suggested that they go on the roof, open up a part it, right above where Jesus was standing. They got some rope and tied it to the four corners of the bed, and with each person holding onto a corner, lowered the bed right down from the roof and it rested right in front of Jesus.

Jesus looked up at the four men and smiled. He was amazed they people believed in him so much to go to all this trouble to see their friend healed.

He looked at the man on the bed, and bend down to look him in the eyes, and he told him "Son, thy sins are forgiven."

But there were in the crowd before him from the synagogue, and they began to whisper between themselves, "How can this man forgive sins, only God can do that." God told Jesus what they were whispering, and stared at them in the crowd. He said, "Why do you doubt the power of God to do anything. Is it easier for me to say, 'Your sins are forgiven', or just 'Take up your bed and walk?' Because God can do anything, he has given the Son of God to act as God on the earth and forgive sins."

Just looked back to him then uttered, "Get up off your bed, and go home." He was cured of paralysis almost instantly, and he jumped up to hug Jesus, crying and thanking him. He got his bed, and pushed his way through the crowd, as people were smiling and hugging him with joy. Astonished, they said, "Wow, we have never ever seen anything like that before."

11. The Faith of the Centurion

And when Jesus entered Capernaum, a centurion came to Him, imploring Him, and saying, "Lord, my servant is lying paralyzed at home, fearfully tormented." Jesus said to him, "I will come and heal him."
(Matthew 8:5-7)

After Jesus was done preaching to the people, a man in a soldier's uniform knocked on his door. He was what was called a centurion, an officer in the Roman army, who had a hundred soldiers following his orders. Jesus invited him in, and the man asked Jesus, "Can you help my servant? He is paralyzed and is very sick and suffering." Perhaps he had heard about the other paralyzed man that Jesus had healed.

Jesus told him, "Sure, I'll come to heal him."

The officer said, "Jesus, I am a worthy that you should even walk into my house. I am a Roman officer, and when I tell my soldiers to march, they do it. When I say to fight, they do it. I have heard you teaching and seen some of your miracles. I have heard of many other things that I wasn't there for, but I believe in everything that you say and do is from God."

Jesus was amazed to hear by a Roman soldier because Jesus was sent to the Jewish people, not to the Romans. They, as well as everyone else who wasn't Jewish, were called Gentiles in the scrolls of God. He wasn't sent to the Gentiles, but there was one who believed totally in what Jesus said and did.

"Jesus, if you just come and heal him, I will believe it."

Jesus had not even seen such believing in the

Jewish people. They all could believe if they saw him perform a miracle, but nobody had yet believed him enough to just believe his words. He told the centurion, that lots of people will come from all over, Jews and Gentiles, but many of even the Jewish people who think they know God will find out someday that they did not due to their refusal to believe the things Jesus said and did. "Since you have believed, even though you aren't Jewish, God sees your believing, and your servant will be healed, ". That hour, the servant of the centurion began to feel better and was healed of all his illness.

Then Jesus left Capernaum and when to a small town called Nain, with his apostles and a large crowd of worshippers following him. There Jesus encountered a burial party, carrying the body of a boy. Most of the little town was following the body. Crying loudly was a widow woman, the dead boy's mother, who had lost her only son. Jesus told her, "Don't cry," and touched him and uttered, "Young man, I say to you 'Arise'", then immediately he rose! Again, many who saw Jesus and knew that the boy was really dead, believed that he was performing miracles.

12. Feeding the Crowd

*And He took the five loaves and the two fishes—
and looking up toward heaven, He blessed the
food and broke the loaves and He kept
giving them to the disciples to set before them;
and He divided up the two fish among them all.
They all ate and were satisfied.*
(Mark 6:41-42)

J esus decided it was time to send out his apostles into different cities so that they could see that they, too, had the spirit of God on them and that they could do the same miracles that Jesus did. He paired them up into six teams and sent them to six different towns. Jesus told them to not take any money or food with them; to not bring any extra clothes with them, either; and to instead let God take care of them along the way.

Jesus also taught them, "Don't worry when you find people who don't believe you. Just shake the dust off your feet and go somewhere else. They can learn about God, and if they don't want to hear, they will have to face the consequences before God someday. It's not your fault if people don't want to believe, it is just your job to speak the truth and let them believe what they want to believe."

The men went out as Jesus had said, and when people heard that they were the apostles of Jesus, they invited them into their houses and feed them and gave them beds to sleep on, so that the men would teach them about Jesus. These six teams went and performed many of the miracles that they had seen Jesus perform, and soon crowds began to follow them as well. They taught the people many of what Jesus shared about God.

Upon returning to Jesus, they were all bubbling with excitement. They all told Jesus of all the wonderful things they have learned and seen, and the miracles that they had performed. Jesus was pleased to see that they learned how loving God is, that God answers prayers if you only believed in Him.

Jesus knew they were tired and asked them to go into a quiet place in the desert, where they could all rest for a while. But the crowds followed them, and soon they were all surrounded by many people. Around 5 thousand people were surrounding them—men, women, and children of all ages. He taught them all day long about God and about how God loves them all and wants to be with them.

When it started getting close to nighttime, the apostles told Jesus that he should let these people find some dinner in the nearby villages. They complained that they didn't have hundreds of dollars to go buy food for all the people.

When the day got late, Jesus asked his apostles,

how much food do you have?

The apostles told him that they only had 2 cooked fishes and 5 loaves of bread. Jesus took the food and told everyone to sit down. They sat down around him in crowds of fifty and groups of a hundred. Jesus took the bread and the fish and prayed that God consecrated the food and divided the bread to smaller pieces and the fish into smaller pieces, and he gave each of his disciples a piece of bread and a piece of fish in the bottom of a basket.

The apostles, just back from seeing themselves perform so many miracles, took the baskets and started passing out pieces of bread and fish from them. Every time they reached into their basket, there were more and more bread and fish in them.

The people surrounded them ate happily, and when dinner was all over, each of the apostles still had baskets full of chunks of bread and fish leftover, even after all five thousand people in the crowd had gotten their fill, both of the bread and fish, and of the word of God.

13. Jesus Walks on Water

And in the fourth watch of the night, He came to them, walking on the sea. When the disciples saw Him walking on the sea, they were terrified, and said, "It is a ghost!" And they cried out in fear. But immediately Jesus spoke to them, saying, "Take courage, it is I; do not be afraid."
(Matthew 14:25-27)

After Jesus had fed the five thousand people, he sent them all home and told his apostles that he wanted to be alone, too. He told them to go rent a boat and go back over the lake to Galilee so that he could spend some time praying to God. Jesus went up into a mountain and watched the sun going down and stared at the beauty of all the stars in heaven. He stayed up all night, praying to God and remembering all the things that had happened to him.

About 3 o'clock in the morning, God told Jesus that his apostles were in trouble and that they needed to be rescued. Jesus immediately departed then headed to the lake and saw that a storm had come in. The wind was very strong, and white caps roll across the water of the lake.

In the middle of the lake, on their rented boat, the apostles were once again being tossed to and fro, up and down, fearing for their lives. The last time, Jesus was with them and he calmed the waters, but this time they were alone. They were very afraid and cried and screamed as the boat rolled back and forth, and big waves splashed water into the boat.

Jesus began to walk across the water, and although his sandals got wet from the waves, Jesus didn't sink. He kept walking until he got close to the boat. The men in the boat saw him coming through the spray of the water and thought they were seeing a ghost walking towards them. They became even more afraid than they were. They thought they were all going to die, right then and there.

But Jesus called out, and said, "Be happy, don't be afraid. It's me!" The men were amazed and very glad that Jesus had come to them. Peter, who was the most afraid of all of them, called out to Jesus to let him walk on water towards him because he just couldn't wait for one more second to be next to Jesus and out of the rocking boat.

Jesus called to Peter, and he stood upright on the lake. Even Peter was shocked. He began to walk towards Jesus, and as long as he stared directly at him, he walked on the top of the water. He got closer and closer to Jesus. But he turned and looked at the boat, now far away and rolling around the in water, and he began to slowly sink. The water covered his toes, and then his knees. He looked back at Jesus and cried, "Jesus, Jesus, save me!"

Jesus reached out and grabbed Peter's hand, and Peter rose up to the top of the water again. Jesus scolded him, "You didn't believe in me, you looked back at the world instead of keeping focused on God to save you."

Then Jesus and Peter walked hand in hand across the water and climbed into the boat with the other apostles. As soon as Jesus stood in the boat, the wind stopped, and the sea began to calm down. The men all around him were amazed once more with all they had seen and said, "You really are the Son of God."

Jesus continued around Galilee, teaching everywhere he went. On one occasion, he told the people that the Word of God was like a farmer throwing seeds out into a planted field. Some of the seeds fell onto stones and dried up in the sun without sprouting. Some fell into the weeds, and they started to grow, but they got choked up by all the weeds. But some fell into the dirt and grew up big and strong. He explained that this was like the Word of God; some refuse to accept it, so these people don't even get the chance to grow. Others hear it, but they refuse to avoid earth's pleasures, so what Word they heard was soon choked out, but some will hear the Word and grow and spread it to others.

He also taught them about the future in a parable. Now, when Jesus taught, he used a lot of what is called, "parables." He could teach his apostles many deep truths about God, but when he was teaching crowds of people he mostly spoke in the form of parables—which is like a fable, a story with a meaning to it in the end, if you think about it. Jesus usually taught about the farmers and fishermen and the world that everyone knew about, in simple words, so everyone could understand him.

Jesus said that when a farmer gathers together his crops, he doesn't try to root out all the weeds first. He gathers both the crop and the weeds together, and sorts out the good food, and burns up all the weeds. This he was talking about man, that God will someday separate out all the good crops from the weeds, and the weeds will be destroyed.

14. The Transfiguration

Six days later, Jesus took with Him Peter
and James and John, and brought them up on a
high mountain by themselves. And He was
transfigured before them; and His garments
became radiant and exceedingly white, as no
launderer on earth can whiten them.
(Mark 9:2-3)

One fine day, as Jesus and his apostles were going around the region of Galilee, Jesus asked John, James, and Peter for them to follow him up into a high mountain. Jesus didn't tell them why, but they were obedient and climbed up the mountain behind him.

When they reached the top of the mountain, Jesus began to glow with a heavenly light. His robe, which was a common brown color used throughout the area, glowed whiter than any white the three apostles had ever seen.

Then Moses and Elishia appeared on either side of Jesus. They glowed with the same heavenly glow and the same brilliant pure white. Above them, a white glowing cloud stopped right over them, and even though the other clouds were moving by in the wind, this one special cloud stayed put. Jesus talked quietly with the two angels beside him about things of God to come.

The apostles became worried and dumbfounded. One of them said, "Jesus, let us take some rocks and make three monuments, one for you and one of both Moses and Elishia." They thought they were doing something good, but they were really just there to witness the events. Then, from the cloud, a mysterious voice emerged, saying, "This is my beloved son; hear him."

The three apostles looked down from the cloud and saw Jesus was standing alone again. The heavenly glow was gone, and Moses and Elishia had vanished.

Upon going down, Jesus asked his apostles to keep what just happened as a secret until he rose—but the men failed to comprehend Jesus.

At that time, Jesus had not taught about his impending death. They thought Jesus would somehow conquer the Romans, take over the country, and rule as the King. They still believed this even up until Jesus said his last words to them.

Jesus knew at that moment, after hearing the whispered promises from Moses and Elishia, that to fulfill all the promises of God, it was to become necessary that he was going to die, but to not be afraid, because God would raise him up again in three days' time. To salvage humankind, he'd have to agonize all the things that the devil was able to throw at him because the devil had always thrown the same things on mankind. But it was Jesus's secret at that moment, and he couldn't tell the apostles because they could not yet understand it.

15. Jesus and the Children

Then some children were brought to Him so that He might lay His hands on them and pray, and the disciples rebuked them. But Jesus said, "Let the children alone, and do not hinder them from coming to Me; for the kingdom of heaven belongs to such as these."
(Matthew 19:13-14)

J esus loved children most of all because they were innocent and so willing to accept love and anything positive. Jesus often used children as an example in his teachings because all they wanted was love and to be taught wonderful things. The Bible used the words "child" or "children" 763 times throughout the Bible.

He taught them that children were the easiest to bring into the Kingdom of Heaven. Now, the

Kingdom of Heaven is not a physical place in heaven itself, but it's a walk on the earth of a person who loves and believes and trusts God. Everyone has a choice to live their life according to God and Jesus and when somebody does that, they can see wondrous miracles in their lives and develop a one-to-one relationship with God.

Then Jesus and his apostles began a trip. They left the region of Galilee, walking to the east, and crossed over the Jordan River.

The religious leaders of the Jews, called Pharisees, came to Jesus to try to trick him into saying something against God. They invented several tricky questions, but Jesus was smarter than all of them and answered every question in such a way that they couldn't accuse him of saying anything wrong.

Then, a group of children was brought to Jesus, even though his disciples questioned why Jesus was blessing babies.

"Permit the children to come to Me, and do not hinder them, for the kingdom of God belongs to such as these. Truly I say to you, whoever does not receive the kingdom of God like a child will not enter it at all."

(Luke 18:16-17)

About this time a man named Jarius came to Jesus to ask for help. Jarius was a ruler in a synagogue in Galilee and he had seen Jesus perform many miracles. Jarius told Jesus that his twelve-year-old daughter, Tabitha, was very sick, close to the point of dying. "Please come to my house and heal her, so she may live," Jarius asked.

On the way, Jesus was followed by a large crowd, and they encountered a cursed woman and couldn't go to worship in the synagogue because of it for twelve years. She believed that healing would come by touching Jesus's robes. When the woman did, He felt the blessing of God going through him, and stopped and turned to the woman and said Who touched my clothes?" The woman admitted she did and told him she thought she could be healed just by touching his clothing. Jesus saw her believing, and said, "Your believing has made you whole."

Jesus continued walking down the street, and men from the synagogue came running up to tell Jesus that Jarius' daughter had just died, and he didn't have to go there now. He told them, "Don't be scared, only believe."

When Jesus got to the house of Jarius, and went into the little girl's bedroom, and said, "Tabitha, wake up." And she did! All the people were astonished at the miracle, but Jesus simply told Jarius to cook something for the girl, because she was hungry.

Jesus always knew that innocent young children were like empty glasses, able to be filled up with whatever their parents put in them. If they were raised with hate and anger and fear, that is how they would live their lives. But if they were filled with love and peace, and the love of a God who cares for them always, they would live their lives that way. Even the old prophets had written that "If you raise up your child according to the Word of God, they will return to it." God didn't promise that they wouldn't stay away from God, but that that foundation would become the bedrock of their lives.

16. The Good Samaritan

But a Samaritan, who was on a journey, came upon him; and when he saw him, he felt compassion, and came to him and bandaged up his wounds, pouring oil and wine on them; and he put him on his own beast, and brought him to an inn and took care of him.

(Luke 10:33-34)

J esus continued to teach parables to the people who surrounded him. One of his parables was about the mustard seed. The mustard is a bush, and it produces seeds that are so very tiny to the point that you can hardly see them. Jesus said that faith or believing is a little one of these little tiny seeds because all you need to have faith in is the truth that everything is possible with God, the Creator. All you need to do is ask and believe in God—and you can move mountains.

One day a man came to Jesus who was trained to study the laws of Moses and to teach the laws to others. He had been sent by the Pharisees to try to trick Jesus, and he asked Jesus directly, "What shall I do to get eternal life?

Instead of answering, Jesus replied, "Well, you study the law of Moses. What do YOU think it says?"

The lawyer said, "Well, Moses wrote to love God with all your heart, and with all your soul, and with all your strength, and love your neighbor as yourself."

He was correct, Jesus said. But then the lawyer asked, "And who is my neighbor?"

Instead of answering the man's question, he began to tell him a parable. Jesus said that a man went south from Jerusalem to Jericho and was attacked and robbed by bandits along the way. They stole his money and his clothes, beat him up, and wounded him on the side of the road.

A synagogue priest came down the street and saw the wounded man on the side of the road, went just across the road and passed him without stopping to see if he could help. Another man, called a Levite, which was a priest who worked in the great Temple in Jerusalem, came by and he also saw the man but just kept riding.

Then came along a Samaritan. Now, the people of Samaria were really not liked by the Jews, because they were poor people who had been imported into the country from the country of Babylon long ago when the Judeans were taken into captivity hundreds of years before. But this man was kind, and went over to the injured man, and wrapped bandages around where he was bleeding, and washed him up with oil and water. Then he helped the man get up onto his horse and drove him to an inn. He rented a room, and cared for the wounded man, bringing him food and water and changing his bandages for him.

The next day, he paid the innkeeper some money and asked that he care for the wounded man until he came back, and he would pay him more when he got back.

When Jesus finished the story, he asked the lawyer, "Now, of the three on the road, the synagogue rabbi, the Temple priest, or the Samaritan who everyone hated, which do you say is the wounded man's neighbor?"

The lawyer looked at Jesus and said, "His neighbor was the one who showed mercy to him."

Jesus uttered, "Go and do so likewise." Hence, what can be learned from this parable is that no matter who you are—rich or poor, smart or foolish—it doesn't matter to God even if you are one of the priests in the Temple, God knows when you love another and when you don't, so love everyone.

17. Mary and Martha

Now as they were traveling along, He entered a village; and a woman named Martha welcomed Him into her home. She had a sister called Mary, who was seated at the Lord's feet, listening to His word.
(Luke 10:38-39)

N ow, after the lawyer went away, Jesus continued walking and came into a small village called Bethany and ran into a woman named Martha. Bethany was nestled in the hills east of Jerusalem, about two miles away. Martha didn't really know who Jesus was, but she invited Jesus to come into her house and have dinner. It was normal for people in those days to invite strangers into their houses and to feed them and give them a place to rest from their journeys.

Martha had a sister, named Mary. Now, Mary had heard of this Jesus, maybe she had even seen him preaching, and she sat Jesus in a chair and she sat on the floor to talk to him. She washed the dust-off Jesus' feet and massaged them with a special expensive rare oil. She even dried his feet with her long hair! This was an act of honor to a special guest in those days.

Martha was inside the kitchen, preparing a meal, and because she didn't know who Jesus was, got upset with her sister for just sitting on the floor while she did all the work. She came into the room and asked Jesus "Can you tell Mary to come to help me cooking, instead of sitting there talking to you?"

Jesus looked at Martha, and said to her, "Martha, Martha, you are all upset with your sister and upset about a bunch of other things, but your sister is going the most important thing she could be doing, by talking to me instead of helping you."

At some point, the women must have sent for their brother, whose name was Lazarus, although he isn't mentioned specifically. He becomes important later in the story but became a good friend of Jesus. Later, Jesus would spend a lot of time together with Mary and Martha and Lazarus in Bethany.

Afterward, Jesus went into Jerusalem to celebrate the holiday of Hanukkah, which is sometimes referred to as Feast of Lights. This holiday celebrated the recovery of the Temple from the Greeks after it had been captured and miss used. Jesus was called in front of the Temple priests again, and he taught some things that tied directly to the holiday they were celebrating:

"I am the Light of the world; he who follows Me will not walk in the darkness, but will have the Light of life." So the Pharisees said to Him, "You are testifying about Yourself; Your testimony is not true." Jesus answered and said to

them, "Even if I testify about Myself, My testimony is true, for I know where I came from and where I am going, but you do not know where I come from or where I going. You judge according to the flesh; I am not judging anyone. But even if I do judge, My judgment is true; for I am not alone in it, but I and the Father who sent Me.

(John 8:12-16)

Later, Jesus was teaching his own followers when he told them, "If you continue in My word, then you are truly disciples of Mine; and you will know the truth, and the truth will make you free."

18. The Lost Sheep

So He told them this parable, saying, "What man among you if he has a hundred sheep and has lost one of them, does not leave the ninety-nine in the open pasture and go after the one which is lost until he finds it? When he has found it, he lays it on his shoulders, rejoicing.
(Luke 15:3-5)

After the Feast of Dedication, Jesus and his apostles traveled through southern Judea, and the Bible records him teaching many parables to the people during this trip. One of Jesus's parables that he used to teach in various ways was about the lost sheep. He used the same parable elsewhere about the lost coin, or the lost son—all of which have the same ending.

Jesus was teaching a group of common people

from the countryside. The religious leaders watched the sermon he gave, complaining that they were the smart religious people, but this man Jesus was always hanging out with a much of sinners. They thought that if he such an important man to God, that he should be spending all his time with the religious leaders. But they wouldn't have believed anything he said, so Jesus preferred to be around people who might be able to learn from him.

Jesus told the crowd that God was like a shepherd that had a hundred sheep, but one of them got lost in the hills. So, the shepherd left his flock with other shepherds, and went out and searched and searched and searched, until he found the lost sheep. He hugged it and led it back to the rest of the flock where it could be fed and protected from wild animals. He was happy that most of his sheep were content to stay where they were safe, but even happier when one strayed away and came back to him.

Then he told them the story of a lost coin. In those days, when a woman got married, she adorned her hair with ten special silver coins, which had hooks attached to them, passed from mother to daughter over generations. When a woman lost one of these coins, she thought that her family would be forever cursed. The woman told her girlfriends, and then swept and cleaned every inch of her house until she found the missing coin. She told all her girlfriends, and they all rejoiced with her that the jewelry was found, and the family wouldn't be cursed. The moral of these stories is that we were all lost to God, and God is overjoyed when we find our ways back to Him.

19. The Lost Son

And he said to him, 'Son, you have always been
with me, and all that is mine is yours. But we
had to celebrate and rejoice, for this brother of
yours was dead and has begun to live
and was lost and has been found."
(Luke 15:31-32)

Then, Jesus continued and told them about a lost son. A man had two sons, and the younger one asked him if he could have all his inheritance. Hence, the man took half of his money and gave it to the younger son, and the son got on his horse and rode far away into another country. Far from his friends and his family, the boy figured that he could do whatever he wanted and that nobody he knew would know about it, so he spent all his money on fancy food and drinking and women and having parties. When he had finally wasted all his money, he had to go out and get a job, but the only thing he could find was a job feeding the pigs. Since he was so empty-handed, he lived on the leftover corn husks of the corn that he fed to the animals. Now, to the Jews, pigs were dirty animals, and they weren't allowed to eat pork or pig meat—or even be around them.

The younger son finally got mad at himself. He said, "I used to be rich in my fathers' house, but here I am feeding pigs, and eating their leftovers." So, he traveled back to his own country, and came to his father's house, crying. He said to his father, "I am so sorry, father. I wasted all the money, and I don't deserve to be treated as your son anymore. Please, can I just be one of your servants?

But the father was so glad to see his son that he thought he had lost forever, he ordered his servants to make a big feast for him. His older brother, however, when he heard what was happening, got mad. He complained to his father that "he always was there, doing whatever the father wanted, but his younger brother had run off and wasted all of his money on parties, and now he comes back, and he gets a big party. It's just not fair!"

The father hugged him and told that he was happy with the son who always was there, but he was very happy that the son he thought was lost and gone forever was saved. This was the meaning of the parables of the lost sheep, the lost coin, and the lost son. So God feels the same way when we go back to Him too.

About this time, the people of Galilee began to talk badly about Jesus. They were amazed about his miracles, but they wondered, "Isn't this the son of Joseph the Carpenter? We know the family; they aren't anyone special. We know all his brothers and sisters; they are just like us. How could this man come out of a common family like that?" When Jesus heard of these murmurings, he simply said, "A prophet can't be respected around his own family or his own town." It's a good lesson in life, that if you change to become a Godly person, your old friends and even your own family might not be able to accept it, because they knew what you were like before finding Christ in your heart. Jesus reasoned that he couldn't do what he now does to his own town, as its citizens had known him growing up.

It was also around this time that trouble was brewing. King Herod, the son of King Herod who had tried to have Jesus killed after he was born, was then the ruler over the Galilee region of Israel. He began to be worried about all the people who were following John the Baptist. King Herod had actually gone to some of John's teachings, and Herod respected John as a man of God, one who taught the Word of God well and with conviction.

20. Lazarus Lives Again

*When He had said these things, He cried out
with a loud voice, "Lazarus, come forth." The
man who had died came forth, bound hand and
foot with wrappings, and his face was wrapped
around with a cloth. Jesus said to
them, "Unbind him, and let him go."*
(John 11:43-44)

Now, one day, Mary and Martha of
Bethany, the same sisters who had
had dinner with Jesus and who Mary
had honored by washing his feet and anointing
them with oil, found out that their brother
Lazarus was dying. They thought that Jesus
could do something about healing him, and they
requested for him to heal their brother in
Bethany. Jesus had become a friend of Lazarus
before and came to heal him.

Jesus had other business to do, so it wasn't for two days that he could be able to leave to go to Bethany. His apostles warned him that people were after him in that area, and they wanted to stone him to death. But he loved Mary and Martha and Lazarus and told them that it was important for him to go to Bethany to help Lazarus.

Jesus told his apostles that Lazarus was sleeping, and they said—if he is resting let him rest. But then Jesus clarified himself, that God had shown him that Lazarus had died on his illness. Then the apostles understood him, and they still feared that Jesus would be captured and stoned to death himself, but they agreed that if Jesus was going to be stoned, they all wanted to go along and be stoned too.

When they got to Bethany, which was a long way away, they came near to the house of Mary and Martha. Mary was sad and stayed inside the house crying about her brother, but Martha ran out to meet Jesus on the road. She told him that Lazarus was dead, and if Jesus had arrived earlier, he could have saved him.

Now, by then, Lazarus had already been dead for four days. His body was wrapped in cloths and placed within a burial cave. In those days. bodies were not buried underground, but into special family caves. They had little shelves built into them, and bodies were placed onto a shelf, and a rock rolled over to cover the entrance of the cave.

Jesus told Martha that Lazarus would live once more. Martha replied, "Yes, Jesus, I know all about the resurrection, when all the dead will live again in heaven." Jesus corrected her, saying he wasn't talking about that resurrection, in the future. But that Lazarus would live again now. He told her:

"I am the resurrection and the life; he who believes in Me will live even if he dies, and everyone who lives and believes in Me will

never die. Do you believe this?"
(John 11:25-26)

Martha said that totally believed Jesus was who he said he was and that God would do anything that Jesus asked for. She sent for Mary, who was still in her house mourning. When she heard that Jesus was on the road outside of Bethany, she ran out of the house, leaving friends behind, to run to Jesus. All her friends followed her, and they were all crying about Lazarus too.

Mary cried out to Jesus, hugging him, and asking him why it took so long. She was a little mad at Jesus, thinking that he would have healed him if he had gotten there quicker. Then even Jesus cried in Mary's arms about his lost friend Lazarus. They went to the burial cave, and Jesus ordered some of the men in the crowd to roll away the stone that blocked it. It smelled really bad there because Lazarus had been deceased 4 days ago. Jesus ignored the smell and then prayed to God out loud:

"Father, I thank You that You have heard Me. I knew that You always hear Me; but because of the people standing around I said it, so that they may believe that You sent Me."

(John 11:41-42)

Jesus cried in a loud voice, "Lazarus, come out!" And then soon, Lazarus appeared from the cave, still wrapped in the burial cloths around his body, and a burial napkin on his face. They helped unwrap Lazarus and dress him in normal clothes.

Many people came to Mary and Martha's house, to hear the wonderful story of how Jesus had raised their brother Lazarus from the grave. But when word got to the chief priests in the Temple, they began to plot Jesus' death. They were scared of anyone who could raise a dead man because they knew they didn't have that sort of power.

21. Bartimaeus Receives His Sight

And answering him, Jesus said, "What do you want Me to do for you?" And the blind man said to Him, "Rabboni, I want to regain my sight!" And Jesus said to him, "Go; your faith has made you well." Immediately he regained his sight and began following Him on the road.
(Mark 10:51-52)

Jesus and his apostles traveled across the Jordan River again, preaching in the Jewish villages on that side of the river, and Jesus began to warn his apostles that there would be a day soon that the government would capture him, torture him, and kill him—but he told them not to be upset, as he promised his resurrection on the third day.

It scared the apostles, and they all swore to him that they would protect him against all those things, even if it meant that had to lay down their lives for Jesus. But Jesus assured them all that it was all written about in the old prophecies of the prophets and confirmed to him by the spirits of Moses and Elisha on the Mount of Transfiguration. They were all concerned about Jesus, but he assured them that he had to be sacrificed to pay for the sins of the whole world.

Now, they crossed over the river again and went along the road from Jericho towards Jerusalem. There, they came across a blind man on the ground, begging for pennies so that he could eat. The name was named Bartimaeus, and he had heard all about all the miracles that Jesus had performed. As Jesus went by, the blind man uttered, "Jesus, son of David, have mercy on me!"

Jesus stopped and called to people in the crowd to bring the blind man to him. They went over to where he was sitting, and helped him up, and led him to Jesus. Jesus looked at him and asked, "What do you want me to do for you?"

The blind man replied, "Lord, that I may receive my sight."

Seeing that the blind man really believed that Jesus was the son of God and that God could do anything that Jesus asked of Him, Jesus said, "Go your way, because your believing has healed you." And immediately the blind man could see.

22. The Conversion of Zaccheus

And Jesus said to him, "Today salvation has come to this house, because he, too, is a son of Abraham. For the Son of Man has come to seek and to save that which was lost."
(Luke 19:9-10)

After Jesus healed the blind man, the group passed by Jericho—and many people lined the road, just for the chance to see Jesus and the apostles pass by. One person in the crowd was a rich tax collector. He was not Jewish and generally hated by the people he had to collect taxes to give to the Romans. However, he had heard about Jesus and wanted to see him for himself.

Unfortunately, when the man whose name was

Zacchaeus got to the road, he couldn't see anything. He was very short, and there were so many people lining the road like a parade that he couldn't see over them. So, he got an idea—he climbed up into a sycamore tree that was close to the road, and from up there he could see above the crowd. Eventually, everyone got excited because they could see Jesus, and the apostles, and a large crowd following them up the road from Jericho.

When Jesus got up to precisely where the sycamore tree was, he stopped suddenly and looked up directly at Zacchaeus. Jesus said, "Zacchaeus, get down out of that tree, and come to me. I am going to spend the night at your house."

All the people watching got a little mad because they knew Zacchaeus was the local tax collector, and they didn't like him at all. Why had Jesus decided to spend the night in his house, they asked?

Jesus and the apostles went with Zacchaeus to his house, and Jesus asked him what sort of man he was. He told Jesus that he was an honest tax collector, he didn't intentionally harm or overcharge anyone, and if he did accidentally, he paid the man back out of his own pocket four times what he had wrongly taken.

Jesus determined that the man would become blessed because even though he wasn't Jewish, he believed in Jesus and he was a descendant of Abraham. His honesty and faith in God would save his whole family from hell. It was a foreshadow of what would happen soon, that even though the Jews were God's chosen people, he loved all the Gentiles as well if they would believe in Him.

Now, after leaving the house of Zacchaeus, the group walked north to the town of Bethany and came to the house of Mary and Martha. Lazarus was there too. Once again, Mary washed Jesus' feet with oil and dried it with her hair. This time, however, Judas was there, and he objected, saying that this oil cost a lot of money—isn't it better to sell it and donate it to the poor, rather than using it to clean Jesus' feet? Jesus replied, "Leave her alone; she is doing this in preparation for my burial. You'll always have poor people, but I won't be around much longer."

23. Jesus Enters Jerusalem

The crowds going ahead of Him, and those who
followed, were shouting,
"Hosanna to the Son of David; Blessed is He
Who Comes in the Name of the Lord.
Hosanna in the highest!"
When He had entered Jerusalem, all the city
was stirred, saying, "Who is this?" And the
crowds were saying, "This is the prophet, Jesus,
from Nazareth in Galilee."
(Matthew 21:9-11)

After the evening with Martha and her siblings, Jesus and the apostles went west towards Jerusalem. When they got to the little village of Bethpage, Jesus told his apostles to go into the village and borrow a donkey—specifically one that has a young baby colt. Jesus knew of an ancient prophet who had written of this moment, who wrote that the King would enter Jerusalem on a donkey, with His son riding on it.

The right donkey was found and brought to Jesus, and they put robes on it for Jesus to ride upon. The crowd that followed him got ahead of him, and laid their clothes onto the road, and cut palm branches down for the trees near the road. This was an event that was prophesied by the prophet Zechariah hundreds of years before, who wrote that "Rejoice greatly, O daughter of Zion; shout O daughter of Jerusalem; behold, the King comes to you; he is just, and has salvation; lowly, riding upon a donkey, and upon the donkey's baby."

Jesus rode towards Jerusalem with everyone cheering and chanting that the new King of Israel was coming into town. This was the event that is still celebrated today as Palm Sunday.

When he got close to it and could see the gates leading into it, he cried, talking about the future destruction of the city by the Romans, saying if you only knew what your future held! The city will be destroyed, not one stone of this Temple will be left on another because you have rejected me.

The next morning, Jesus and his followed entered Jerusalem, and Jesus was hungry. He saw a fig tree in someone's yard, and couldn't find any figs on it. Fig trees at the time were considered the "people's fruit", and it was acceptable for a stranger to take a fig off the tree to eat. But this one only had leaves, not figs. Jesus looked at the tree and said, "No fruit will ever grow on this tree." Jesus was actually talking about the Jews in the city, who had failed to believe when the Messiah was there and that they too were soon going to wither away. This is exactly what happened. In the year 70 AD, the Romans destroyed Jerusalem, wrecked the Temple so not one stone sat on another one, then scattered the Jews all over the Roman Empire, and it wasn't until 1948 that Israel became a country again.

24. Trouble in the Temple

And Jesus entered the temple and drove out all those who were buying and selling in the temple, and overturned the tables of the money changers and the seats of those who were selling doves.
(Matthew 21:12)

J esus went straight towards the Temple that King Herod had built and came into the street leading towards its entrance. There were booths that had been set up by people who could change the Jewish money into Persian coins because the Jewish money was nearly worthless, and the Persian money had become the only coins that the priests of the Temple have decided to accept for donations. Because of having to change from one coin to the other, the Jewish people lost money every time they came to the Temple to worship, while the moneychangers and the priests got rich.

There were also people in the booths selling animals for the sacrifices. These were sickly lambs and doves, that the merchants bought for a few pennies, and sold to the worshippers for a lot more. Why not? they thought, they were only going to be killed soon afterward anyway. There was also a constant haggling going on between the moneychangers and the sellers of sacrificial animals with their customers, that nobody could hear the services in the Temple.

When Jesus entered the street, God showed him that every one of the merchants there were only thinking of their own greed. None of them were honestly selling anything that pleased God. Jesus became enraged for once in his life, with a rage that God felt towards them, and knocked over the tables and cursed at the men, calling them evil and that they don't deserve to be doing anything in God's Temple.

Jesus cried out "My house is supposed to be an example of God to all the people in the world, but you have turned it into a den of thieves."

Children were still calling out "Hosanna, the King of the Jews." The chief priests of the Temple were angered by Jesus coming in like he owned the place and that the children were calling out to worship him. They went to Jesus, and asked, "Do you hear what the children are saying?" Jesus looked at the priests and said, "Out of the mouths of babes and suckling, there is perfect praise."

After leaving the Temple, Jesus and the apostles returned to Bethany. The next morning, they passed by the fig tree again and saw that it had completely withered away.

When they got to the Temple, the priests there tried to accuse him of blaspheming God, a crime there punishable by death. This was an attempt by the priests to get evidence on him to charge him with this crime. It failed, but before the priests left Jesus told them four parables about them. Two of the parables were about a vineyard, and two about a marriage feast, so they could see what their conduct looked to Jesus and to God. Instead of being faithful workers for God, they were behaving as self-serving, wicked servants and false prophets.

After leaving the Temple, Jesus met with his apostles on the Mount of Olives. There they questioned him about the end times. Throughout his ministry, everyone around him had expected his to be a conquering king, to rid them of the Roman government controlling Israel, and establish his own kingdom. It was finally becoming apparent to all of them that it was not the time for that to happen.

They asked, "Tell us, when will you come back to set up your kingdom, and what will be the signs of your second coming?"

Jesus told them, "Nobody knows the hour, except for my Father. There will be wars and rumors of wars, and the days will become like the days of Noah when everyone does what he feels like doing without any obedience to God or His word. But watch like a watchman, and you'll know when the days are close."

He also told them about the Rapture of the believers from the world. He said there will be a day when two people are working in the field— one is taken, and the other is left behind. And two women working together milling grain, when one is taken and the other is left. This Rapture will happen to remove all of God's children off of the world—before the devil gets his final chance to ruin it

Then, Jesus told his apostles about several parables to help them understand more clearly. One was about ten unmarried women. They went out to meet their future husbands, carrying lamps. But five of the women were foolish and didn't put oil into their lamps. The other five were wise and filled their lamps before they went out. The foolish women were locked out of the room because they were not properly prepared. God wants us to always be ready for Christ to come back for us.

The second parable was about a rich man and his servants. The rich man gave coins to three of his servants, according to how well he trusted them. To one he gave five coins, to another two coins, and to the third one coin. Then the rich man went on a trip. The servant with the five coins used them to trade for other items, and when the rich man returned, the servant had doubled his money. The servant with the two coins also doubled the man's money and was praised. The man who only had one coin had buried it, and could only give the man back the same coin he had been given. The rich man took his coin away and gave it to another. Jesus said the lesson of this parable is that God came into the world to give mankind an opportunity to prosper—but if you are lazy and disobedient and fail to believe in God, in the end, you may end up losing everything.

25. The Last Supper

*While they were eating, Jesus took some bread,
and after a blessing, He broke it and gave it to
the disciples, and said, "Take, eat; this is My
body." And when He had taken a cup and given
thanks, He gave it to them, saying, "Drink from
it, all of you; for this is My blood of the
covenant, which is poured out for many for the
forgiveness of sins."*
(Matthew 26:26-28)

Now, Jesus met with his apostles to share their last meal together at Martha's house in Bethany, on the Sabbath before the Passover holiday. It would begin the last week of Jesus' life on earth. All twelve of the apostles were with him.

A typical meal in Israel at the time consisted of a sort of a stew, with whatever meat they could afford, and a mixture of vegetables, cooked over an open fire. Everyone would sit on the floor, around a low table that was only maybe six inches off the floor. Their bread was not like modern bread, but a flatbread like what we now call pita bread. Spoons had not yet been invented, so this stew was poured into bowls, and then pieces of the pita-type bread would be broken off and used to dip into the stew to get the food.

Jesus was teaching them that every time they ate a meal, they should remember him, and how he was soon going to give his own body to be broken to pay for all the illnesses that a man can have. So, he took his bread, and tore it into small pieces, and handed each of his friends a piece. He prayed thanks to God, and He told them, take this and eat it, and you will remember my body which will become broken for you.

Then he took his wine glass, it may have been a glass or even a clay cup because both were common at the time. He took his cup, prayed for that too, and told his men to take their cups of wine and take a sip, to remember that I must shed my blood for the removal of sins too.

Throughout the Old Testament, people have sacrificed animals as a payment for sin. The earliest recorded was when God told Abraham to take his only son Isaac up into a mountain to sacrifice for Him. Abraham assumed that it meant he had to sacrifice Isaac to God, but God supplied a lamb instead. During the first Passover, Moses told the Israelites to sacrifice young lambs and sprinkle its blood on the doors so the angel of Death would go over their houses. Throughout all the years of the Temple, the priests sacrificed lambs or small pigeons.

His men didn't fully understand what he meant by all these things, because they hadn't been told exactly all what was going to happen, but they remembered what he told them afterward, and the practice of the holy communion is still practiced in the church today. But the deeper meaning that Jesus was teaching was to remember his sacrifice at every meal you have, breakfast, lunch, and dinner, and always be thankful that God can forgive your sins if you ask Him.

During the meal, Jesus and Judas Iscariot both reached into the pot at the same time, and Jesus said that Judas was going to betray him. Judas had already gone to the chief priests in the Temple and told them that he would betray Christ for thirty silver coins. Jesus didn't know that, but God told him.

After they had eaten, Jesus poured a bowl full of water and washed each of the apostle's feet. This was a symbol of service to them. Peter objected, saying that the Master should not be washing the servant's feet. But Jesus told him that it was a lesson to all of them, that God wants to us be servants to all mankind, and bless and teach everyone about God.

Then the apostles and friends sat around him as Jesus began a long teaching just for their ears. In it, he told them some wonderful things about God. He said that he was preparing a place for all of them in heaven, and someday they would see the wonderful mansions for them to live in forever. He said that they had all seen God because Jesus did all the works of the Father during his ministry on earth. And he told them there would come a day soon that the Holy Spirit would come to all of them, and they could do the same sorts of miracles that they had seen Jesus do, and even great things because Jesus was returning to God. He said that this Holy Spirit would be a great comforter to them, to whisper the words of God to them.

Finally, at the end of the teaching, Jesus prayed for them a wonderful prayer. He thanked God for their lives and all they had been through together. He prayed that they would remember his words, and spread them out into the entire world after he was gone. He prayed that they would live their lives close to the heart of God—like Jesus had lived his life—and be forever blessed to serve God. Some of the most memorable words Jesus spoke were in this prayer, to his apostles but also to all of us today:

"Do not let your heart be troubled; do believe in God, and believe also in Me. In My Father's house are many dwelling places; if it were not so, I would have told you; for I go to prepare a place for you . . .. Believe Me, that I am in the Father and the Father is in Me; otherwise believe because of the works themselves. Truly, truly, I say to you, he who believes in Me, the works that I do, he will do also; and greater works than these he will do; because I go to the Father. Whatever you ask in My name, that will I do, so that the Father may be glorified in the Son. If you ask Me anything in My name, I will do it…. "If anyone loves Me, he will keep My word; and My Father will love him, and We will come to him and

make Our abode with him . . .. Peace I leave
with you; My peace I give to you; not as the
world gives do I give to you. Do not let your
heart be troubled, nor let it be fearful. You heard
that I said to you, 'I go away, and I will come to
you.' If you loved Me, you would have rejoiced
because I go to the is greater than I . . .. I am the
true vine, and My Father is the vinedresser—
for the Father. Every branch in Me that does not
bear fruit, He takes away; and
every branch that bears fruit, He prunes it so
that it may bear more fruit. You are
already clean because of the word which I have
spoken to you. Abide in Me, and I in you. As the
branch cannot bear the fruit of itself unless it
abides in the vine, so neither can you unless you
abide in Me. I am the vine, you are the
branches; he who abides in Me and I in him,
he bears much fruit, for apart from Me you can
do nothing.... If anyone does not abide in Me, he
is thrown away as a branch and dries up . . ..
Just as the Father has loved Me, I have also
loved you; abide in My love. If you keep My

*commandments, you will abide in My love; just as I have kept My Father's commandments and abide in His love. These things I have spoken to you so that My joy may be in you, and that your joy may be made full. "This is My commandment, that you love one another, just as I have loved you. Greater love has no one than this, that one lay down his life for his friends.... This I command you, that you love one another. **(John 14:1,2; 11-14; 27-28, John 15:1-5; 9-13, 17)***

Later that night, Jesus took his apostles from Martha's house in Bethany, over the Mount of Olives and down to the hill on the other side of the Temple, to a beautiful garden called Gethsemane. He told them to wait there for him, and they all sat down among the flowers, but Jesus told Peter, James, and John to follow him. Jesus was very sad and quiet as they walked farther up the hill. Then Jesus told them to wait and watch out for him, so they sat down also, while Jesus went still a little further.

Jesus got on his knees, and then laid all the way down with his arms stretched upon the ground as he prayed to God:

"My Father, if it is possible, let this cup pass from Me; yet not as I will, but as You will."
(Matthew 26:39)

Jesus knew from the scriptures of the prophets and from what God had told him that he was soon going to have to go through the most horrible torture and death that any man had ever gone through. Of course, he didn't what to have to go through it, but he believed that God would give him the strength he needed to get through it, and God's greater purpose for his life would soon make it all worthwhile. While he hoped for any other way to accomplish the goal of freeing mankind from all its sins, he accepted that if it was God's will that he went through it, he would.

His apostles had fallen asleep, so he woke them up and they all returned to Bethany and went to bed in Martha's house.

26. Mocked

And after twisting together a crown of thorns,
they put it on His head, and a reed in His right
hand; and they knelt down before Him and
mocked Him, saying, "Hail, King of the Jews!"
They spat on Him, and took the reed
and began to beat Him on the head.
(Matthew 27:29-30)

Judas, the betrayer, wasn't there but had left after dinner and met with the priests and had schemed with them that he would identify Christ to the soldiers that came to arrest him by giving Jesus a kiss on the cheek.

At midnight, Jesus awoke as Judas came marching down the road with the priests, and the elders of the city, and a large group of soldiers carrying swords and poles with metal arrowheads on them. When Judas got up to

Jesus, he kissed him on the cheek, and immediately the soldiers moved up to arrest Jesus. Peter pulled out his sword and cut off the ear of one of the soldiers arresting Jesus. But Jesus healed the soldier right on the spot and told his apostles that it was all going on as God had told him it would and that if he had really wanted to stop this from happening, God would send him thousands of angels if he asked for them.

So, the soldiers and the priests led Jesus away and took to a highly respected man named Annas, who said to send the prisoner to his son-in-law, the chief priest of the Temple, Caiaphas. Caiaphas asked him about what things Jesus taught, and Jesus told him that he had taught all about God and heaven and had always taught in the open. He said that everyone knew what he taught already, so why are you asking me this question—when you already know the answer?

One of the soldiers slapped Jesus across the face

for talking back to the High Priest, and they tied a blindfold over his eyes and hit him in the face and made fun of him. Caiaphas ordered that Jesus is brought before the council of Temple priests.

The Council chambers of the Sanhedrin, known as the Hall of Hewn Stone, was on the south-west corner of the Temple grounds. They were the most learned men of Jewish law and met together to make decisions about violations of Moses' laws. Now it was long after midnight, and the Sanhedrin had to all be woken up and come to the Hall under the cover of darkness.

They questioned Jesus, to try to find a legal way to have him executed. A number of people came by, to say that Jesus did this or that, but it was all according to God's laws. Finally, they brought in two witnesses, who said that Jesus had threatened to destroy the Temple in three days and that he was the Messiah, the Son of God. The Sanhedrin found Jesus guilty of treason and blasphemy against the church and said that he was worthy of death. But Caiaphas didn't want to be responsible to kill him directly, so he sent Jesus to the Roman governor of Judea.

The Judgment Hall in Jerusalem was the palace of the Roman Governor. It had a large mosaic floor from out the Hall, which is mentioned in the Bible. It was early in the morning, with the sun just coming up. Because it was the morning of the Passover holiday, which would begin at sundown, the members of the Sanhedrin would not go inside the palace but asked the governor to come out to them. The Roman governor was a man named Pontius Pilate. Pilate asked what charges they had against this Jesus. They replied that Jesus was a criminal, the Sanhedrin wasn't allowed to execute anyone, only the governor could sentence him to death.

Pilate took Jesus into the Judgment Hall, and questioned him, "Are you the King of the Jews?" Jesus replied that he was a king, but not of the current world and time. Pilate decided there was no reason to execute him, and went out to tell that to the Sanhedrin outside. The Jews were upset, but when Pilate heard that Jesus had mostly taught in the Galilee, he decided to send his to the overseer of that region, King Herod.

Herod was glad to see Jesus, having heard many wonderful things about him, and hope to see Jesus perform some miracles for him. But Jesus just stood there silently, making Herod mad. He sent Jesus back to Pilate.

It was a tradition then that he would release one prisoner out of two, just before the Passover, and let the Jews decide which one to let go. Pilate wanted to let Jesus go free, but he was bound by rules not to allow that. So, he got a vicious murderer out of jail, named Barabbas, and offered to the crowd which had formed to let one go, and to kill the other one. He figured that Barabbas was so very bad, there was no way the people would choose him to be freed. In the back of the crowd, the priests began to chant, "Kill Jesus, kill Jesus", and soon the entire crowd was chanting it too. So, Governor Pilate went over to a bowl of water and washed his hands and told the crowd that his blood would be on them. He would do as they asked and kill Jesus and let Barabbas go free.

Then the soldiers of Pilate took Jesus into a large hall in the governor's house, and stripped off his clothes, and put one of the governor's scarlet colored royal robes on him. One man ran outside and got a piece of a bush with long, strong thorns on it, and they put it around his head like a crown and twisted the ends together until the thorns cut deeply into his head, and blood began to drip down his hair and face. But Jesus just stood silently and proudly.

Then they found a thick stick and placed it in his hand, and the soldiers bowed down in front of him, making fun of him, saying "Hail, King of the Jews." They all took turns spitting into his face, and hitting him all over with the stick, and punching him in the face. Then the soldiers took a whip, with long leather strips that had broken bones or glass or sharp metal tied on the ends, and beat Jesus with it. The sharp ends would cut into his skin and rip big chunks out of his back and stomach and arms and legs. It was terribly painful, but Jesus just stood there and never said a word. Soon Jesus was bloody and bruised all over, with big bruises on his eyes and nose and mouth, so that he hardly even looked human now.

Pilate brought the bloody Jesus out again before the Priests, hoping that they would have compassion on the man. They just said, "Crucify him, crucify him." Pilate led Jesus out again before all the people, and told them "Behold your king!" They answered, "We have no king but Caesar, crucify him!" So Pilate was forced to order it, and they led Jesus away to be executed.

Jesus stood tall and proud for all the abuse. He

knew must go through all the torture, worse than any man ever had, to pay the price for every time anyone is abused, or called bad names, or made fun of, or beaten in life. Jesus went through it all, so we can all stand proud too when all the evils of the world try to beat us down. Because Jesus went through it all for us, we can stand proud through anything too, knowing God is with us.

27. The Crucifixion and Death of Jesus

And when they came to a place called Golgotha, which means Place of a Skull, they gave Him wine to drink mixed with gall; and after tasting it, He was unwilling to drink. And when they had crucified Him, they divided up His garments among themselves by casting lots... And Jesus cried out again with a loud voice and yielded up His spirit.
(Matthew 27:33-35, 50)

Now, after the soldiers had mocked Jesus, they put his real clothes back on him and led him away to be crucified. It's not used anymore, but crucifixion was a way the Romans used to kill their slaves who had committed serious crimes. It was to be a warning to other slaves to be obedient to their masters. A large tree was firmly planted onto the ground, and then a prisoner had his hands nailed to a board, with his arms stretched high and wide. Above that board was another, with the crime they committed written on it. The prisoners were usually forced to walk from the prison to the place of hanging with the board nailed through their hands so that everyone could see them being led to their death. The board was then nailed to the tree, thus making a cross. The prisoner would hang on the board until he died from starvation or being strangled.

Two other criminals were also led from the prison towards the execution place. Jesus was too badly beaten to walk with the board, so the soldiers grabbed a man from the crowd, who was there to celebrate the Passover, and made him carry the board through the streets of Jerusalem, His name of Simon, a Cyrenian.

The soldier's led Jesus up to the place on the east

side of the Jordan River, across from the Temple, at a place called the Place of the Skull. There is still a rock formation there that does look just like a skull. They took some water mixed with something that was supposed to help the prisoner not feel as much pain while he was dying, but Jesus tasted it and spit it out and refused to take any more of it. He had to go through the entire thing without a sedative.

So, they removed his outer clothes, leaving him in only his underwear, and nailed the board to the tree. A large crowd gathered to watch it happen, including his own mother, Mary. The solder's nailed other criminals to the trees around Jesus, too.

Since it was Passover, ready to start in just a few hours, many thousands of people had come to the Temple to worship God. From the Temple, you can see across the Kidron Valley to the Place of the Skull, where Jesus was hanging. Jesus was quiet and peaceful, while everyone else around him was crying. His own mother, Mary, was there shaking and crying, as were many other of his friends and family.

The priests took another board, and wrote on it: "Jesus of Nazareth, King of the Jews" and had it nailed above his head. The soldiers laughed at Jesus too, saying things like, "If you are really the King, call on God to get you off the cross!"

As Jesus hung on the cross, one of the others who was sacrificed with him asked him "Can you save me too?" Jesus told him, yes, I promise you today, that I will see you in paradise." The others hanging there laughed at him, but Jesus was promising that when the earth became a paradise again, at his first Coming, that man would be raised from the dead and have eternal life.

Suddenly, the skies grew dark with thick clouds, and it was like night time from about 3 o'clock to 6 o'clock. After the clouds moved away, the priests began to tell the soldiers that they had to kill Jesus because it was getting close to nighttime, and they couldn't allow him to hang there once the Passover meal was started. One of the soldiers took a spear with a long metal arrowhead on it and shoved it into his belly just below his ribs, far up to pierce his internal organs. Jesus began to bleed heavily from the wound.

As he stood there exhausted, he cried to God, "My God, my God, for Your purpose I have given my life." A few minutes later, Jesus died on the cross.

Right after he died, Jerusalem was hit by a strong earthquake, and the crowd watching the crucifixion and all the worshippers in the Temple fell onto the ground. Inside the Temple, a thick curtain that covered the Holy of Holies was torn in half from the top to the bottom. Many people there said, "Truly, this was the Son of God that was just killed."

Jesus died at the beginning of the Passover, as the perfect Passover sacrifice, the perfect Lamb, the perfect Adam, who was wounded to pay for all the sins of mankind. Beaten and bruised, mocked and spit on, Jesus endured everything a man could ever go through, so he would be the perfect payment in full for all the sins of mankind since Adam first sinned. Jesus was the perfect Passover lamb, paying for sin not just for one year, but for all time. Now, we can go to Jesus when we sin, and ask him to forgive us of those sins too. And in the future, Jesus can lead us to heaven as spotless and pure, to enter into paradise forever.

28. Jesus Is Risen

The angel said to the women, "Do not be afraid; for I know that you are looking for Jesus who has been crucified. He is not here, for He has risen, just as He said. Come, see the place where He was lying. Go quickly and tell His disciples that He has risen from the dead; and behold, He is going ahead of you into Galilee, there you will see Him; behold, I have told you."
(Matthew 28:5-7)

A rich man named Joseph of Arimathea, who had a burial cave nearby, and one of Jesus's disciples, went to Mary, Jesus' mother, and told the family that Jesus could be laid to rest in his burial cave. His burial cave was nearby, and it had been freshly dugout and didn't have any other bodies in it. They agreed, and Joseph had the body taken down off the cross and wrapped in a clean white linen cloth and placed into Joseph's wagon. The family followed the wagon to the burial cave, and the body was placed inside on one of the burial niches. Mary and the others went to Jerusalem to buy spices and oil to prepare the body and soon returned to put them on the it. When they were done, a large stone was rolled over in front of the cave to seal it off. The crowd cried as the burial was happening, including Mary Magdalene and Mary, the mother of Jesus.

The next day, the Jewish priests came to Pontius Pilate and asked that he guard the grave, fearing that someone might steal the body and hide it, and they might try to say that Jesus had risen from the dead. Pilate ordered his soldiers to seal up the stone at the burial cave, so it couldn't be opened and set guards there to make sure nobody came close.

A few days later, on Sunday morning, Mary

Magdalene and Mary, the mother of Jesus, walked down to the grave cave. There was another earthquake, and an angel appeared, and the stone rolled away from the cave. The soldiers guarding the cave passed out cold from the sight of the angel. When the women got there, the angel said to them, "Jesus isn't here, he has risen from the dead. Go look inside the cave for yourself."

They went into the cave and saw the linen burial cloth and the cloth they had laid over his face, just lying on the shelf with nobody inside it. They came out and the angel said, "Go back to Galilee, that's where you will see the risen Christ."

Mary turned around and saw a man standing there that she assumed was a gardener because she didn't recognize him. She asked if he had seen anyone come and steal the body of Jesus out of the cave. The man just said, "Mary" and she immediately recognized the voice, and knew it was Jesus, risen from the dead. She wanted to run over and give him a big hug, but he told her not to touch him, as he first had to go to heaven and present himself to God.

29. Doubting Thomas

But Thomas, one of the twelve, called Didymus, was not with them when Jesus came. So the other disciples were saying to him, "We have seen the Lord!" But he said to them, "Unless I see in His hands the imprint of the nails, and put my finger into the place of the nails, and put my hand into His side, I will not believe."

(John 20:24-25)

Now, when Mary went back to the apostles, she found them all hiding in the upper room of an inn. They were all afraid that the priests would be coming after them, too. She told the apostles that they had seen the angel of God, about seeing Jesus, about the Angel, about the empty tomb, and about the fact that they were all supposed to go back to Galilee and that there they would all see the risen Jesus Christ. However, the apostles still couldn't believe the things that Mary said were really true.

The next day, two of Christ's disciples were walking from Jerusalem to a small village nearby called Emmaus. As they cried and talked about the horrible execution of Jesus, another man came up behind them and asked why they were so sad. They said, "Are you a stranger here, didn't you see what happened in Jerusalem a few days ago?" The stranger asked, "What things." The men told the stranger all about Jesus, and his ministry, and his miracles, and what horrible things were done to him, and the things that Mary had told them about the empty tomb and seeing the risen Christ.

Then, as they walked along, the stranger told the two all about the ancient prophecies that had been written about the Messiah, and they thought he was a wise man, and invited him to come to their house and have dinner. He agreed, and as they broke bread together, their eyes were opened and they realized that this was the risen Christ they had been talking to. And then Jesus vanished out of their sight.

The next day, as the apostles were still gathered together in the upper room of the inn, Jesus appeared to all of them himself. He said, "Peace be unto you," and he showed them the wounds on his hands where they were nailed to the cross, and the wound on his stomach that had been pierced by a spear, they were all amazed and happy to see him.

Jesus asked, "Do you have anything to eat?" They gave him a piece of a broiled fish, and a section of sweet honeycomb, dripping with honey. Then he taught them that very soon they would be able to receive the Holy Spirit into themselves, and when they saw the tongues like fire, they were to breathe in deeply.

After Jesus left, one of the apostles, Thomas,

showed up. He wasn't there to see Jesus, told everyone else that he didn't believe it. He said, "I can only believe it if I can see it for myself, with my own eyes."

Eight days later, they were still all locked into the room waiting to return to Galilee. Jesus appeared to them again and focused his attention this time on Thomas. He told him to look at his hands, so see the holes left by the nails and to stick a finger into the holes. And Jesus said to reach into his stomach, to see for yourself that it is the actual wound from the cross.

Thomas did as Jesus said, and was finally convinced that this could only be the risen Christ. He told Jesus, "My Lord and my God."

Jesus looked at him, and making sure that everyone could hear him, Jesus said, "Thomas, because you saw me, you believed. Blessed is everyone who can't actually see me, but still believe in me." He was talking about you and me because we can't see Christ, but we can still believe!

After they saw Jesus in Jerusalem, they all returned to their own homes in Galilee. Jesus continued to appear to them, to teach them things they needed to know. On one occasion, Peter and Thomas and other apostles and disciples were together on the Sea of Tiberius, the Roman name for the Lake Kinnereth. They were all together to go fishing all night but didn't happen to catch anything.

The next morning, Jesus appeared to them all by the seashore, and called out "Do you have anything to eat?"

They answered no, and Jesus told them to throw out their fishing net. They did, and when they pulled it back out of the water, it was full of fish. They came back to shore, and started a fire, and had a wonderful breakfast together of bread and fried fish.

Those scriptures give us a clue what living will be like in our own future. We will have wonderful eternal bodies like Jesus now has. We will be able to be with our friends and family. We will still eat and be able to enjoy each other's company. We won't be floating around in the clouds, but walking on the earth enjoying it as it is turned back into Paradise.

30. The Ascension

And after He had said these things, He was lifted while they were looking on, and a cloud received Him out of their sight. And as they were gazing intently into the sky while He was going, behold, two men in white clothing stood beside them. They also said, "Men of Galilee, why do you stand looking into the sky? This Jesus, who has been taken up from you into heaven, will come in just the same way as you have watched Him go into heaven."

(Acts 1:9-11)

For a total of forty days, Jesus appeared to the apostles in Galilee and taught them those things they had to know to carry on his mission on earth. He also appeared before Peter and James—and at least once in front of a crowd of five hundred of his followers

Finally, Jesus knew it was time for him to leave the earth. He told the apostles to go back down to Jerusalem and meet them on top of the Mount of Olives.

When Jesus appeared before them on the Mount of Olives, on a fortieth day after the crucifixion. Jesus told them that it was time for him to leave. All the apostles were there, except Judas. Jesus told them that they all had a special mission:

"You will receive power when the Holy Spirit has come upon you, and you shall be My witnesses both in Jerusalem, and in all Judea and Samaria, and even to the remotest part of the earth."
(Acts 1:8)

"Go therefore and make disciples of all the nations, baptizing them in the name of the Father and the Son and the Holy Spirit, teaching them to observe all that I commanded you; and lo, I am with you always, even to the

*end of the age." (**Matthew 28:19-20**)*

After Jesus had taught them all about the Holy Spirit to come to them, he promised them, "I am with you always, until the end of the world." Then he told them to walk with him down the mountain on the road towards Bethany.

As they walked, the apostles asked him, "When are you coming back to conquer the Romans and take over as the eternal King?" Jesus told them all that the time was a secret, and nobody knew the hour but God. But until then, they were all to go back to Jerusalem and wait for the sign of the Holy Spirit, to receive the Holy Spirit and teach the whole world about him. They were, "to be witnesses of him to Judea, and in Samaria, and unto the uttermost parts of the earth." Even then, the apostles didn't realize that he meant to teach not only the Jews—but to everyone else, too.

When he was done saying these things to them,

Jesus was lifted into the clouds and disappeared. The men all stared upwards at the cloud in amazement, but they looked and found that two men were standing there in pure white robes. They knew they were angels.

The angels told them, "Why are you staring up into the sky? This same Jesus will return one day in the same way."

So, the apostles returned off the Mount of Olives to Bethany and then went to the room that they had rented in Jerusalem and waited for the sign of the Holy Spirit from God that Jesus had promised to them.

This completed Christ's personal ministry on the earth. Although the four gospels contain many wonderful things about him, it was written that there were so many other things that he did that weren't written down that the world couldn't even hold all the books that could be written about it. But the gospels were sufficient for people to know that Jesus was the Christ, the Son of God and that anyone can have eternal life by believing in his name.

31. The Holy Spirit

When the day of Pentecost had come, they were all together in one place. And suddenly there came from heaven a noise like a violent rushing wind, and it filled the whole house where they were sitting. And there appeared to them tongues as of fire distributing themselves, and they rested on each one of them. And they were all filled with the Holy Spirit and began to speak with other tongues, as the Spirit was giving them utterance.

(Acts 2:1-4)

Now, the next week was a special one called Pentecost. It was another one of those Jewish holidays when everyone was supposed to come to Jerusalem and worship at the large Temple there. It was celebrated fifty days after Passover, called

Pentecost, or the Feast of the First Fruits, because it celebrated the first of the crops being ready to eat. Since Jesus was the Passover lamb for all eternity, they would celebrate the First Fruits of the Holy Spirit on that day.

The apostles rented the same room that they had before in Jerusalem, in the upper floor of an inn, where Jesus had previously shown himself before them, and to Mary, and to the doubting Thomas. Mary came there to visit them, and they had meals together and discussed Jesus and all they had seen and heard.

While the apostles were at Jerusalem, they decided that they had to appoint a new disciple to fill Judas's place among the twelve leaders of the group. Judas had killed himself because he was so sad about having betrayed Jesus. Judas had taken a sword, and stuck it into the ground, and fell on it so that his insides came out. The priests had him buried in the same poor peoples' cemetery that the priests had bought with the 30 pieces of silver they had bribed Judas with.

The apostles called a meeting of the disciples, who numbered about 120 people, and picked out two of the strongest believers they knew, Joseph and Matthias. The crowd voted, and they picked Matthias to become the replacement for Judas.

The city of Jerusalem was very crowded with people who came for the Pentecost celebration, and there was hardly any room to move about the outer courts of the Temple. On the day of the Pentecost celebration, the apostles all went to the Temple together, to worship according to Jewish law. They found an open spot and seated down in a circle. Suddenly there came a sound like a rushing mighty wind, and the apostles looked up and saw what looked like a ball of fire coming down from heaven. As it neared them, twelve tongues came out and stood above each one of their heads.

They knew this was the sign from God that Jesus

had told them about. They all took a deep breath and began to speak in other tongues. Some were earthly languages; some were speaking the language of the angels. The languages kept changing, and all the people around them heard the twelve apostles praising God in their own language.

There were Parthians, Medes, Persians, Egyptians, Libyans, Crete, Arabians, and many others—and they all heard the men speaking in their own language. Many were amazed to hear these men of Galilee praising God in their own language, speaking the wonderful works of God. It was amazing!

The visitors all around the apostles stood dumbfounded, with their mouths open. Some people just cried out that they were drunk. When Peter stood up and cried out "Men of Jerusalem, and Judea, and around the world, don't be shocked. We aren't drunk, it's only noon. No, no, this is what was prophesied hundreds of years ago by the Prophet Joel, that God would pour out His Holy Spirit unto anyone who believes in Jesus Christ, the risen savior of man.!"

32. New Recruits

And with many other words, he
solemnly testified and kept on exhorting them,
saying, "Be saved from this perverse
generation!" So then, those who had received his
word were baptized; and that day there were
added about three thousand souls. They
were continually devoting themselves to the
apostles' teaching and to fellowship, to the
breaking of bread and to prayer.
(Acts 2:40-42)

O n the day of Pentecost, Peter went on to teach everyone about Jesus Christ and his ministry on earth, of salvation, shaking a fist at the ones in the crowd who had called for Jesus's death. He taught everyone that God had raised Jesus from the dead, that he is now Lord of the Universe and the Christ and the

Messiah that everyone had looked forward to for millennia.

Peter told them that King David had also prophesied about Jesus. David had written that he believed in the Messiah and that he knew he would die someday but that a Messiah would be born and David would be raised from the dead to live with the promised Christ. And this Jesus, who was recently killed, was that risen savior and is both Lord and Christ.

"Men of Israel, listen to these words: Jesus the Nazarene, a man attested to you by God with miracles and wonders and signs which God performed through Him in your midst, just as you yourselves know— this Man, delivered over by the predetermined plan and foreknowledge of God, you nailed to a cross by the hands of godless men and put Him to death. But God raised Him up again, putting an end to the agony of death since it was impossible for Him to be held in its power. For

David says of Him,

'I SAW THE LORD ALWAYS IN MY PRESENCE;
HE IS AT MY RIGHT HAND SO THAT I WILL NOT BE
SHAKEN.
'THEREFORE MY HEART WAS GLAD AND MY TONGUE
EXULTED;
MOREOVER, MY FLESH ALSO WILL LIVE IN HOPE;
BECAUSE YOU WILL NOT ABANDON MY SOUL
TO HADES,
NOR ALLOW YOUR HOLY ONE TO UNDERGO DECAY.
'YOU HAVE MADE KNOWN TO ME THE WAYS OF LIFE;
YOU WILL MAKE ME FULL OF GLADNESS WITH YOUR
PRESENCE.'

Brethren, I may confidently say to you regarding the patriarch David that he both died and was buried, and his tomb is with us to this day. And so, because he was a prophet and knew that GOD HAD SWORN TO HIM WITH AN OATH TO SEAT one OF HIS DESCENDANTS ON HIS THRONE, he looked ahead and spoke of the resurrection of the Christ, that HE WAS NEITHER

*ABANDONED TO HADES, NOR DID **His flesh** SUFFER DECAY. **This Jesus God raised up again, to which we are all witnesses. Therefore, having been exalted to the right hand of God, and having received from the Father the promise of the Holy Spirit, He has poured forth this which you both see and hear. (Acts 2:22-33)***

Three thousand men and women in the audience believed the words of Peter, and the church began on that day. The apostles divided everyone into groups, and with the other elder disciples who had personally been with Jesus, began to meet in smaller groups to share meals together and to tell the new believers all about the things Jesus had taught them during his ministry, and all the wonderful things they had personally witnessed.

They continued to grow, passing the message of Christ from one house to the next, sharing meals, teaching, and singing praises to God. Many even gave everything they had to the needs of the growing church, so food and clothing and such could be bought for the new believers who needed anything. As the apostles went out, the message of Jesus Christ was passed throughout all the land of Judea, into the cities of Galilee and Samaria, and into the countries that surrounded them.

One day, Peter and John went to the Temple to worship, and they encountered a lame man sitting near the Beautiful Gate. There was a high wall around Jerusalem, with twelve gates around it, each with a different name. The man was sitting there, begging for food, and the apostles saw him and taught him about God and Jesus and told him, "In the name of Jesus Christ of Nazareth, rise up and walk."

They helped the man up, and as he rose, his legs were healed. He ran into the Temple, leaping, and praising God. He hugged Peter and John, and the people around them were amazed. Peter began to preach to the crowd, "Why are you all so amazed? The God of Abraham and Isaac can do anything and healed him. And Jesus, who YOU crucified, an innocent man, died to pay for all YOUR sins. Now, repent of your sins and come back to God." After Peter's sermon, more people repented of their evil ways and turned to follow after Jesus.

The early days of the church were not all joy and happiness. Some people still had too many of their old, evil ways about them. One example was Ananias and his wife, Sapphira. They had a piece of land and told the church that they were going to sell it and give the money to the apostles to help spread the Gospel. They did sell it but kept part of the money for themselves. For this, the apostles called them out as liars against God. It wasn't that they kept some for themselves that was wrong, but the fact that they were so boastful about their charity to the church. Ananias was so grieved about being caught in a lie, that he walked out of the room and died.

As the church expanded around Jerusalem, the apostles began to get into more and more trouble with the Temple priests and elders, the same evil ones which had been directly responsible for crucifying Christ. The apostles were arrested, but an Angel came and unlocked the doors and let them out. The apostles came right back the next morning and taught in the Temple, right before the priests.

The priests met, and had the apostles brought to them again. They were very mad at them. The priests said, "You have filled up all of Jerusalem with this doctrine, and you are trying to bring Jesus's blood on us."

Peter spoke angrily for the group, and said, "We ought to believe God rather than man. YOU did crucify him, and YOU hung him on the cross! But God raised him up from the dead to be the ultimate payment for sin, and to bring the Holy Spirit, and we are witnesses to the fact that the things we say are all true."

One of the Pharisees there, a man named Gamaliel, very intelligent about the laws of the Jews, took the Priests aside and told them, "Leave these men alone. If it is all just an act or a lie, nothing will come of it. And if it really is from God, nothing you can do will stop it." The priests agreed and after they had the apostles beaten, they told them all to not speak in the name of Jesus anymore, let them go. Of course, the apostles went right back to preaching about Christ, going from house to house to meet with the believers meeting in their homes.

Most of the recorded expansion of the Christian church is attributed to the Apostle Peter. In one early episode, a disciple that was known as Philip the Evangelist went to Samaria to teach Christianity. A great many people were healed and believed, but nobody was being born again. It was a mystery to Philip what was happening. Then he encountered a man named Simon, a magician, who had bewitched the people there.

Philip was able to cast out his devils and convert him to Jesus as well, and many were baptized. Peter and John came up to Samaria to see what the problem was, and after they had laid hands on the people, they also finally received the Holy Spirit.

The apostle Peter was directed to go to a house of a Gentile in the city of Caesarea and teach him about Jesus. Caesarea was a port city on the Mediterranean, built by King Herod, and mostly filled with Roman citizens. Peter objected to it because he still thought that Jesus had only been sent to the Jews. Jesus came to him in a dream, showing a large net filled with all sorts of animals, including some which were considered unclean by the Jews. Jesus told him that what God cleaned, was clean, no matter what the Jews taught. So Peter agreed and went to the home of Cornelius, a Roman soldier. Peter taught him and his family about Jesus, and after he taught, the whole family got born again and began to speak in other tongues. Peter was amazed to see that the Gentiles too could receive the Holy Spirit as he had. This was the first time that Gentiles had been brought into the promised family of God.

The other apostles were at first mystified by the news when Peter told them about it. It went against everything they had ever believed. But Peter convinced them, saying, "What was I, that could withstand God?" After that, they glorified God, that he would give the Gentiles repentance unto eternal life also.

Now the church was expanding to the Gentiles as well, and King Herod began a persecution of the Church. He had James, the brother of John, killed. Then he had Peter arrested, and put in prison. An angel came and broke him out in a miraculous manner. He was being guarded by sixteen soldiers, and at night, they chained Peter to men on either side of him. The angel removed the chains in the middle of the night and Peter walked right out of the prison.

Peter and the other apostles continued to go from synagogue to synagogue, and from house to house, preaching the words that Jesus had taught them about. Many miracles were done before the Jews of the day. But there was even more to come.

33. The Conversion of Saul

*So Ananias departed and entered the house, and
after laying his hands on him said, "Brother
Saul, the Lord Jesus, who appeared to you on
the road by which you were coming, has sent
me so that you may regain your sight and
be filled with the Holy Spirit." And immediately
there fell from his eyes something like scales,
and he regained his sight, and he got up and
was baptized.*

(Acts 9:17-18)

One day, the priests captured the apostle named Stephen and brought him to the same courtroom to have him accused of blasphemy against the Temple— it was the same place that Jesus had been accused. Stephen gave them a long lecture about the ancient prophecies, how over and over again the people of the land promised to Abraham had rejected the words of the prophets. He talked about how Abraham and Isaac looked forward to the coming King and how Moses walked with God and how he had to deal with people all around him who were constantly rejecting God. Finally, in a fit of righteous rage, Stephen yelled at the priests:

You men who are stiff-necked and uncircumcised in heart and ears are always resisting the Holy Spirit; you are doing just as your fathers dd. Which one of the prophets did your fathers not persecute? They killed those who had previously announced the coming of the Righteous One, whose betrayers and murderers you have now become; you who received the law as ordained by angels, and yet did not keep it."
(Acts 7:51-53)

Stephen told them, "Now, you priests have rejected God and killed his son." Then. he looked up with sharp eyes and told the priests that he saw the heavens open and saw a vision of God, with Jesus sitting on the right hand of God. When he said that, it was the final straw! It took a toll on the said priests, as what he had just said jeopardizes everything they have believed in and everything they have done thus far—and they, being egotistical, self-righteous, unconscienced, mean, power-hungry men, they would not let Stephen get away with what he had dared to say and do.

After all that, the priests were enraged and had Stephen taken outside the city walls. They surrounded him, took off their coats, and put them in a pile before one of their young men. They threw stones at Stephen, who prayed, "Lord Jesus, receive my spirit." Then, he knelt down and said, "Lord, lay not this sin to their charge," and he died.

In the crowd, the young man watching over the priests' things was named Saul. He did not join in stoning Stephen, but he wondered about all the things that Stephen has said to them about the truth that the priests have so conspicuously denied and got enraged about.

Now, as the apostles and disciples spread the word far and near, word got back to the priests at the Temple and the Roman government that a group had continued to grow, and had become so big it could challenge their authority. Although Rome allowed many pagan religions to be practiced through their kingdom, when it came to these new people, who called, "Christ-Ins", because they were always preaching about Christ being in them.

It scared the Temple priests especially. Among them was a man named Saul, who had been raised in the synagogues of the Jews and was an expert in what the ancient texts, called the Torah, said. He was the same young man who was there when the apostle Stephen was stoned to death by the High Priests of the Temple and watched it all happen.

Saul was tasked by the Temple and the Roman government to track down where these Christian meetings were being held and to surround it with soldiers, and break into their houses to take everyone prisoners. Men, women and even children were arrested and jailed for practicing this outlawed religion.

Saul was committed to doing his job, thinking that he was right for trying to stop this new religion from growing. As the new Christians were terrified, they left their homes and spread out into other countries. This only helped to spread the news of Jesus Christ to other lands and other peoples. Soon people were becoming Christians throughout the entire eastern Mediterranean area.

Saul went to the Temple priests and asked them to write a letter of introduction for him, so he could go up to the country of Syria, where some of these Christian fellowships were being held.

Since he was working outside of his own country, the letter was asking the government in Syria to allow him to arrest these people and take them back to Jerusalem.

He proceeded with a group of soldiers and the letter in hand towards the capital of Syria, Damascus. As he got close to Damascus, a voice cried out from above, saying "Saul, Saul, why are you persecuting me?" Saul fell on the ground, asked who it was, and the voice told him it was Jesus.

Saul asked, "What am I supposed to do?"

Jesus told him to go into Damascus and wait there. When Saul tried to stand up, he found that he was blind. The soldiers helped lead him into the city and to find an inn to stay in.

Then Jesus came to a believer in Damascus named Ananias, in a dream. Jesus told him to go to the Street called Straight, and there find a man named Saul and baptize him. Ananias objected, saying that he had heard of this man, who had come to Damascus to capture and tie up the Christians there and carry them back to the High Priests in Jerusalem. He was afraid to do what Jesus asked.

Jesus answered him in the dream and told him not to worry, but Saul was a chosen vessel for him to bring Christianity to the Gentiles. Ananias agreed, and the next morning, when he woke up, he went to the Street called Straight and found the inn run by Judas and came to Saul.

Ananias witnessed to Saul, and told him all about Jesus Christ, what he had said and done, and what all the old prophets had said about the coming Messiah. Saul was very well educated about the Law and the Prophets—and eventually, Ananias was able to convince him that this was the man was the foretold Messiah. When Saul was finally able to believe, Ananias laid his hands on Saul, and immediately he was healed on his blindness. Ananias then baptized him, and Saul received the Holy Spirit.

Saul became really excited about Jesus Christ, and after returning to Jerusalem, he met with the apostles and the other church leaders, but people were afraid of him. They doubted that he was a Christian, but just trying to fool them so he could arrest them. Eventually, the apostles advised Saul to go far away, into a city called Tarsus in Turkey, and begin teaching the Jews there about Jesus Christ. Since nobody knew him there, he could witness to people and they would become Christians too.

Years went by, and eventually, people forgot about the bad things Saul had done. Saul changed his name to Paul, and the Apostle Paul became one of the most important teachers and writers of the early Christian church, writing many of the letters that became part of the New Testament.

Paul greatly preached around the eastern

Mediterranean, to spread the word of Christ to the Gentile nations. He traveled to Antioch in Syria, to Cyprus, to Galatia, then up to Galatia

When Paul was in Galatia, he was called by Peter to return to Jerusalem. The Christians there were still having an issue with the fact that Gentiles were entering the Church, that the Word of Christ was not only for the Jewish people. These objections were mostly coming from Temple priests who had been converted to Christianity but still held on to their old feelings. The leaders of the Christian church held a meeting, and Peter was able to tell them all directly what wonderful miracles he had seen about the Gentile converts. James, the brother of Jesus, determined that Peter instruct them against some practices that were in violation of the laws of Moses, to appease the Jews there, and to just be joyful that God had permitted the Gentiles to be added to the church.

Paul continued to teach, through Thessalonica

and Corinth in what is now Turkey, and later in Athens in Greece. During these travels, Paul commonly wrote letters to the churches throughout Asia Minor, which were voiced by the Holy Spirit. These letters became what is known as the Epistles in the New Testament. Paul had befriended a great ally, a young man named Timothy, who spend much of Paul's later years traveling with him and presumably helping Paul translate his writings from Hebrew into the common Greek of the Gentile lands.

Paul was often arrested, threatened, stoned, lost at sea, but he always relied on God. Eventually, Paul was imprisoned for years. He ended up in Rome and rented a house there for two years. It is likely that during that time, with his good friend Timothy, he translated the gospel accounts of Jesus written by the apostles from Hebrew into Greek, so the Gentiles could read them also.

Paul continued to travel around Asia Minor until

he got old, seeing a great expansion in the Church and correcting problems as they arose. As he got towards his death, the last letter that he wrote was to his good friend, Timothy. The letters to Timothy were full of great secrets about God and Christ because Paul trusted Timothy greatly to understand and teach what he wrote. His very last words voiced Paul's belief that Jesus Christ would return someday to wake him from death, and he would be made incorruptible:

I solemnly charge you in the presence of God and of Christ Jesus, who is to judge the living and the dead, and by His appearing and His kingdom: preach the word; be ready in season and out of season; reprove, rebuke, exhort, with great patience and instruction. For the time will come when they will not endure sound doctrine; but wanting to have their ears tickled, they will accumulate for themselves teachers in accordance to their own desires, and will turn away their ears from the

truth and will turn aside to myths. But you, be
sober in all things, endure hardship, do the
work of an evangelist, fulfill your ministry. For
I am already being poured out as a drink
offering, and the time of my departure has
come. I have fought the good fight, I have
finished the course, I have kept the faith; in the
future there is laid up for me the crown of
righteousness, which the Lord, the righteous
Judge, will award to me on that day; and not
only to me, but also to all who have loved
His appearing.

(II Timothy 4:1-8)

34. I Am Coming Soon

*"Behold, I am coming quickly, and
My reward is with Me, to render to every
man according to what he has done. I am
the Alpha and the Omega, the first and the
last, the beginning and the end."*
(Revelation 22:12-13)

W hen Christ ascended to heaven, he promised to return someday as Lord of Lords and King of Kings. Many, many people believed on his promises but eventually died—knowing that he would come again soon and raise them all from the dead.

The return of Jesus Christ hasn't happened yet, but it *will* someday. His return will happen in two parts. First, he will appear in the sky to bring home to him all those people who ever believed on him and were born of the Holy Spirit. Great trumpets will sound in the sky—and at the last trumpet, first, all those people who have died will be charged from dead, corruptible bodies into incorruptible ones. Then, all those who are still alive will be changed, in the blink of an eye, from mortal to immortal people. Then, everyone will rise together and meet Jesus in the sky. We will all go to heaven together and be with Jesus Christ forever.

When we get there, we will all stand before the bema seat of Christ. The bema seat is not a seat of judgment—but the word was used in the Greek language as the award platform during the Olympics. Christ will personally reward us for our lives offered to Him and give us jeweled crowns. We will know our old family members and friends and spend eternity together with our loved ones and make new friends, too.

Once all the Christians are taken off the world, a

terrible time will come for those who are left. The Devil will be able to do whatever he wants for a period of seven years, inflicting great pain on everyone. Terrible natural disasters will happen all over the world—but God has also appointed people to become new Christians during this time and bring as many people as they can to the knowledge and love of Jesus Christ. It is terrible that they must go through these horrible times, but God had promised that they, too, would live again with Christ.

Finally, at the end of the seven years, Christ and all the believers in heaven will go back to earth—and as one mighty army, they would defeat all the evil people and the evil spirits on earth. The devil will be chained up for a thousand years. Then, all the new believers from the last seven years will also be raised from the dead, and Jesus Christ and all the believers will live together on earth for the next thousand years as immortal souls, enjoying life together, rebuilding the earth back into a paradise like the Garden of Eden.

At the end of the thousand years, Satan will be released for a short time, but he will be conquered and thrown into an eternal lake of fire. God, who is all perfect Love, would even give the devil one more chance to repent and come back to God. However, the devil would instead make war against all of God's people, and God will cast him into a burning pit of fire—to be punished for all eternity.

Then, God would raise up every other person who had even been born and judge them according to their works. He would grant eternal life to people who had not heard of Christ but had done their best to be good to raise their families well. Those who had been hateful, mean people—God would make them vanish forever.

Then, God promised what the future of all eternity would be like:

*Then I saw a new heaven and a new earth;
for the first heaven and the first earth passed
away, and there is no longer any sea. And I
saw the holy city, new Jerusalem, coming down
out of heaven from God, made ready as a bride
adorned for her husband. And I heard a loud
voice from the throne, saying, "Behold, the
tabernacle of God is among men, and He will
dwell among them, and they shall be His people,
and God Himself will be among them, and He
will wipe away every tear from their eyes;
and there will no longer be any death; there will
no longer be any mourning, or crying, or
pain; the first things have passed away."*

*And He who sits on the throne said, "Behold, I
am making all things new." And He said,
"Write, for these words are faithful and
true." Then He said to me, "It is done. I am
the Alpha and the Omega, the beginning and the
end. I will give to the one who thirsts from the*

spring of the water of life without cost. He who overcomes will inherit these things, and I will be his God and he will be My son....

Then he showed me a river of the water of life, clear as crystal, coming from the throne of God and of the Lamb, in the middle of its street. On either side of the river was the tree of life, bearing twelve kinds of fruit, yielding its fruit every month; and the leaves of the tree were for the healing of the nations. There will no longer be any curse, and the throne of God and of the Lamb will be in it, and His bondservants will serve Him; they will see His face, and His name will be on their foreheads. And there will no longer be any night; and they will not have need of the light of a lamp nor the light of the sun, because the Lord God will illumine them; and they will reign forever and ever (**Revelation 21:1-7 and 22:1-5**).

Jesus Christ will rule this new *Jerusalem* forever—as King of Kings and Lord of Lords—and we will be forever by His side.

Conclusion

Thank you for making it through to the end of *The Bible Story Book For Kids*. Let's hope it was informative and able to provide you with all of the tools you need to achieve your goals—whatever they may be.

My little children, wherever you are, God is with you. Although you can't see God with your eyes or touch Him with your hands, you know that He is present with the joy and goodness in your life. You can talk to God without speaking a word. Just by thinking gratefully, you can talk to Him about the majesty of the stars, about the light and comfort of the sun and the moon, about the gracefulness of the birds and the beauty of the flowers, the freshness of cool water, the purpose and friendliness of your animal friends. You know that God hears you—by the fun you have at play, by the good food and loving care that He provides for you, and by the reward of happiness you receive when you are kind and considerate of others. May your daily prayers to God and gratitude for your blessings help you to always understand the power of knowing that God is with you—*always*!

Ultimately, may this book lead you to an understanding of God and of His son, Jesus Christ, to the point that you believe and confess Christ to be your personal savior—that you are filled with the Holy Spirit and given the promise of everlasting life.

"THE WORD IS NEAR YOU, IN YOUR MOUTH AND IN YOUR HEART"—that is, the word of faith that we are preaching is that if you confess with your mouth Jesus as Lord and believe in your heart that God raised Him from the dead, you will be saved—for with the heart a person believes, resulting in righteousness; and with the mouth he confesses, resulting in salvation.
(Romans 10:8-10)

If you have any questions about what you have read, ask your parents or guardian. They will be happy to talk about it with you!

Praise God and his son, Christ Jesus, Lord of Lords and King of Kings.

Amen!